D0556070

This book is dedicated to moms – everywhere.

Guilt-Free Mommy

Insights and Tools
to Overcome Mommy Guilt

Dayna Reed

Copyright © 2020 by Dayna Reed

All rights reserved.

No part of this book may be reproduced or used in any manner or by any means, electronic or mechanical, including photocopying, recording, or by an information storage and retrieval system, without written permission of the copyright owner.

ISBN: 978-1-7347596-0-0 (paperback)
ISBN: 978-1-7347596-1-7 (ebook)

Library of Congress Control Number: 2020904826

Printed in the United States of America

First Edition, 2020

Cover Illustration and Design by Meera Lee Patel

Book Formatting by Ebook Launch

www.guiltfreemommy.com

Contents

1: Identifying the Problem 1

2: Uncovering the Problem 9

3: The Many Faces of Mommy Guilt 19

4: Child Care 49

5: On Being Selfish
   (AKA Caring for Yourself) 91

6: A Spiritual Take on Things 111

Final Thoughts 143

Dear Reader,

Many years ago, I embarked upon the magical journey of motherhood, eager yet pretty naïve as to what awaited me. It would turn out to be an adventure that would challenge, shape, and change me like no other.

As with most new moms, helpful advice from others was never in short supply. But out of all the tips I received, not one person warned me about the slew of sources that would open the door to the unwelcome bouts of guilt I would experience and the uncertainties regarding parenting that would ensue.

With no one else talking about this type of guilt, I was left feeling alone as I battled it. Not wanting to bother anyone with my issues, I resolved to deal with it on my own. That is, until a number of serendipitous events revealed that my situation was hardly unique.

These revelations got me to wondering: *If I've been trying to brave it out by tackling this problem alone, how many other moms are doing the same?* It was this question that set my focus on exposing and defeating this aggressor.

Cue the birth of Guilt-Free Mommy

Just what is a Guilt-Free Mommy? First and foremost – she's free! Free from concerning herself with the criticisms of those who try to dictate how she should raise her children. She's confident as a mom, forgoing the constant need to consult with others to see if she's "doing it right." She has eliminated negative self-talk over her parenting mistakes because, well, she's human. Besides, those mistakes were never intentional. In a nutshell, she trusts her God-given maternal instincts to know what's best for her children and unapologetically raises them with that in mind.

By sharing how I've been able to defeat mommy guilt, I intend to shed some light on ways that you too can become free from the many "guilts" that afflict us moms.

~

Either you've picked up this book because you're well-acquainted with mommy guilt, or I've stirred some intrigue within you. Regardless of the reason that brought you here, welcome! What you'll find within these pages are events and stories that I've experienced over the past twenty years surrounding mommy guilt, as well as the methods to conquer it that I discovered along the way. Some content might be familiar to you, other parts entirely new; what's certain is that the time has come to evict this nuisance, and I'm here to share how. Now let's dig in.

Welcome Back?

It's still fresh in my memory: returning to church after giving birth to our first child, Jaicie. My husband Franklin and I were so excited for everyone to finally meet our baby girl. We arrived a little after the service began, so most of our friends would have to wait a while to get a closer look. Throughout the service, other moms periodically glanced our way with bright eyes and enthusiastic smiles, appearing just as ecstatic as we were about our new addition.

Things took a turn, however, when feeding time came and I pulled out the Avent baby bottle. As I sat there feeding my baby, I noticed a few of those warm looks strangely turn to scowls. Somewhat puzzled, I looked around, wondering if I'd missed something that was said, not realizing that those frowns were meant for me. The service couldn't have ended fast enough for some of those moms to make a beeline to where we were sitting. But it wasn't so that they could finally meet Jaicie or greet me. Instead, it was to grill me with questions such as:

> *"What's with the bottle?!"*
> *"You aren't nursing?!"*
> *"Well, are you at least pumping?!"*
> *"Please tell me that's not formula in that bottle!"*

I was so caught off guard by the ambush that my initial response was shocked silence, followed by: "Whoa...Wait a minute! What?!" My happy moment quickly deflated and I felt as if I'd shifted from being in the House of the Lord to the courtroom of Judge Judy.

What they didn't know was that I'd had an emergency C-section followed by a tough recovery, and my new baby was a bit colicky – all factors that had led to my decision to discontinue nursing earlier than I'd hoped. And although things hadn't worked out quite the way I had planned, everything was still good: my baby was healthy, I was healing, and we were happy!

Needless to say, I left church far from uplifted that day. Instead, I left feeling discouraged and questioning everything I had done for my baby those past couple of months. Although I'd been able to shut down the interrogation successfully at the time, the uncertainty their words produced and the feeling of having failed lingered for days to come. I desperately wanted nothing but the best for my baby. I began to wonder if I was giving her that.

~

I didn't know it then, but this wouldn't be my last encounter with this incriminating analysis over how I cared for my children or the second-guessing it created within me. In fact, it was only the beginning, and would unexpectedly grow into something more troubling than I could imagine. Something, my friend, I would eventually come to know as *mommy guilt!*

1

Identifying the Problem

What is Mommy Guilt?

Mommy Guilt – The widely felt but often undisclosed feelings of guilt that moms experience when trying to live up to the unrealistic and often unattainable external and internal expectations of parenting.

~

No, mommy guilt is not a figment of your imagination. It's real and runs rampant throughout mommydom. In fact, you'd probably be hard-pressed to find a mom who has never experienced it. Although this type of guilt is rife in the lives of many moms, it often goes undetected, as most mothers don't usually identify what they're experiencing as "guilt," leaving them subject to its disturbing nature. Either that or the sensation is disregarded as insignificant or swept under the rug out of embarrassment, causing moms to suffer silently, thinking they're alone in experiencing it.

Well, you're not alone! No matter how intense or mild the feeling is or how frequent or sporadic the episodes, at some point, and to some degree, moms from all walks of life have sensed the influence of this invisible bully. It has become such a common occurrence that many moms think there isn't much they can do to resist its advances. While it is true that moms tend to be the parent that most often falls prey to this type of guilt, it's equally true that it doesn't have to defeat us.

~

I'm quite familiar with the confidence-crushing effects of mommy guilt. I've had my fair share of its many silent-but-sharp mental attacks that convincingly list the numerous reasons why I sucked as a mom, and the judgmental words of others that made me feel the same way. At one point, I too accepted this harassment, thinking it merely came with the territory of being a mom. I dealt with it until I'd had enough of the yo-yo effect it had on my emotions. This aggravation was what produced a determination in me to do something about it.

Eureka!

That day at church was my first memorable brush with mommy guilt. However, not yet having a name for it and not recognizing the behavior, I endured it. Little did I know that there would be many more occasions when it would crop up. It wouldn't be until some ten or so years later that I'd realize mommy guilt was a real issue for other moms as well. I had to literally go back to elementary school, of all places, to recognize its inner workings – my youngest daughter Justyce's elementary school, that is.

~

As the other moms and I waited for the final bell to ring and the kids to pour out of the doors, a daily practice of ours was to chitchat about this and that. The conversations began lightheartedly but, as we became more familiar with one another, we'd increasingly swap comments along the lines of, "I feel so bad about needing to go back to work," or "Aren't I the worst for missing my child's school performance?" Although these comments were made somewhat jokingly, after a while, I picked up on an underlying anxiousness within those moms – mainly because that same unrest was in me.

Curious, I began doing some digging. I started by asking family members, close friends, and other moms I knew if they also wrestled with mommy guilt. As I suspected, all (that's right, *all!*) of them responded with a resounding *yes*. Some moms, also unaware that it was guilt they had been experiencing, were glad to finally give it a name, while other moms were surprised and even relieved to learn they weren't the only ones being bothered by it. I then asked them to write down the specific instances when the cloud of guilt would appear to see if there were any commonalities – and there were.

It troubled me seeing so many moms waste time and energy on this peace stealer. As there was for everything in life, I knew there had to be a way to overcome this. Finding that solution became my mission.

Getting Started

Our mission together is clear: freeing you from mommy guilt. For some, this might seem insurmountable after having grappled with it for so long. At least, that's how I felt. Something in me knew it wouldn't simply go quietly into the night; instead, overcoming it would require a great deal of stick-to-it-iveness on my part.

Ridding myself from the guilt was two-fold: it involved first recognizing the outside triggers that set it off but, even more than that, it called for introspection, which meant starting with the woman in the mirror. I needed to figure out why I continued to allow the accusations to affect me, which required taking a close look at myself.

I began by asking myself lots of questions . . . honest, soul-searching, and, at times, downright hard questions, then staying around to discover the sometimes even harder answers. These Q & A's – which challenged my self-trust, mindset, actions, motives, aspirations, and especially spirituality – were the main keys to my freedom as they exposed the insecurities, fears, and intentions from which the guilt was able to grow. They were aids that helped me recognize and ultimately eliminate thoughts, feelings, and behaviors that encouraged mommy guilt. Now, don't get me wrong, even today there are times when the guilt attempts to creep back in, only now I'm able to spot it and block it before it gains momentum.

It was also important for me to understand that not all feelings of guilt were wasteful, negative, or intended to be condemning. Guilt, in some instances, can be useful. Being armed with this knowledge was helpful in correctly recognizing and responding to mommy guilt.

~

In the same manner in which I questioned myself, I will pose questions for you to ponder. I will not necessarily provide all of the answers, however, because I believe that seeking out solutions that resonate and align within you is the most rewarding part of the discovery.

This work is an "inside job." A baring of your soul to yourself, so to speak, where you turn the spotlight inward and get to know and understand yourself a little better. As such, this might be a bit uncomfortable in the beginning, but nothing worth having – in this case, restoring your confidence as a mom and peace of mind – comes without some discomfort. You'll discover that your satisfaction with your outward display as a mom is proportionate to the degree that you engage in this inner work.

~

Let me reassure you; this isn't a book giving more "rules" for moms to live by, the majority of which promote the very guilt we need to defeat. We've had enough of those! Instead, it's a toolbox of sorts to help identify and demolish unhealthy thought structures or behaviors surrounding motherhood that give rise to feelings of guilt. It will also permit you to reject the pressure of trying to live up to the "perfect mom" image that exists today – because we've also had enough of her. And while our lips say, "There's no such thing as a perfect mom," our actions prove that we yet strive to become her.

~

Mothers, and women in general, hold a tender place in my heart. We have been entrusted with the wonderful gift of bringing forth life and nurturing that life to its fullest potential. My desire is for you to stop berating yourself and to enjoy the richness of this gift of motherhood as fully as possible, which includes being free from mommy guilt and shifting from the practice of criticizing one another to becoming our sisters' keeper.

Without personally knowing each of you reading this book, I know that you are beautiful, sufficient, needed, and loved. Believe this!

2

Uncovering the Problem

Distinguishing the Guilt

Guilt is a complex emotion that can be brought on by different stimuli. Consequently, not all guilt is created equal. Yet, many people view and go about resolving each occurrence in the same way. If we are to defeat mommy guilt successfully, we mustn't only identify it, but accurately differentiate it.

A couple of familiar terms used to describe the way we experience guilt are "guilty conscience" and "guilt trip." Although some people might use the two terms interchangeably, they aren't synonymous. One can be helpful and the other harmful. As such, let's become clear about the type we're out to eliminate.

Guilty Conscience

Remorse caused by feeling responsible for some offense.

- The Free Dictionary

A feeling of guilt experienced by someone who is aware of having done something wrong.

- Collins English Dictionary

Have you ever mistreated, spoken rudely to, or lied to your child (or anyone for that matter) and later felt awful about it? You can accredit that heavy sense of remorse to your conscience at work. A **guilty conscience** emerges when your actions clash with your moral code. Your conscience nudges you, calling your attention to those breaches that, if repeatedly ignored, can cause you to become callous over time.

Being called out on one's errors isn't exactly enjoyable. As such, the discomfort that accompanies these nudges may be misinterpreted as a personal attack, causing you to shun or feel guilt at its appearing. However, this gentle prod comes to instruct, prompting you to correct a situation that's gone wrong.

~

Guilt Trip

1. To make others feel guilt, especially in an attempt to manipulate them.

2. A feeling of guilt or responsibility, esp. one not justified by reality.

 - The Free Dictionary

Guilting yourself as a form of self-punishment for a purported wrong you've committed.

 - Dayna Reed

The guilt that moms most often experience falls under the label of **guilt trip**. This type of guilt can be a bit trickier to detect. While external sources often initiate it, their manipulative rhetoric can gradually become lodged in your subconscious and resurface as your own thoughts. You then begin to feel attacked externally and internally, as you're troubled from both fronts.

The external guilt inducers – be they family, friends, neighbors, society in general, or even your child – readily share their opinionated and, at times, judgmental views of your parenting decisions with hopes that you'll respond in a way that pleases them. And because they can, at times, display a solicitous demeanor, you may lower your guard, welcoming the influence of these sources.

The internal guilt inducer is a component of your ego (i.e., your personal sense of identity). This particular part of your ego has been bruised by the past offenses it has endured in life, some of which have never completely healed. As a result, this bruised portion of your ego – which I call your *inner mean girl* – takes the negative opinions hurled at you by others (as well as your own parenting slipups), internalizes and magnifies them and, by unleashing accusatory inner chatter, convinces you of your insufficiency as a mother. These allegations can seem to spring into your mind out of thin air, but they aren't arbitrary at all. They're sparked by those very same opinions that call into question your effectiveness as a mom – opinions that you begin to believe.

From thoughts such as:

- "You're not as good a mom as she is."
- "You're selfish."
- "A good mom would *never* do _____." [fill in the blank]
- "That decision you made (for your child) screwed up their life.

To thoughts causing you to feel guilty about:

- Being a single or divorced parent.

- Not having the means to buy your children things they want.
- Not feeding your children organic food.
- Going out with friends.
- Wanting some alone time.
- Disciplining your children.

To feeling guilty about:

- Being a stay-at-home mom.
- Working outside of the home.
- Returning to work after maternity leave.
- The decision to put your children in daycare.
- Not spending enough time with your children.
- Working too much.

The list can be a mile long.

Nearly all of the above have nagged me. These guilty thoughts can appear when you least expect them, such as while having a conversation with someone, observing another mom interact with her children, watching a TV show or movie, or surfing the internet. Therefore, you seldom challenge the validity of these intrusive thoughts. Why? Well, because they sound like you. They manifest inwardly, in your voice, your tone, and your speech pattern, making them sound credible. Plus, there's usually some truth mixed into the accusation, causing you to conclude that they must be right. Right? Wrong!

Things changed for me when I realized that the accusations were sure to come no matter what; it was what I *did* with these accusations when they appeared that made all the difference. And, regardless of the source, these thoughts could only affect me if I agreed with them. I didn't have to allow them to escort me down a path of emotional distress. Instead, I had power over them. Understanding this was a turning point for me.

Knowing there were going to be times when I had to put in extra hours at work or times when I not only desired but needed some "me time," I had the choice of either sinking below the waves of guilt or anchoring myself with clear intent and purpose for my actions. I chose the latter.

~

We began this chapter distinguishing between the friendly nudges of our conscience and guilt trips. As we progress, one of our objectives will be to discern and desensitize ourselves from the latter while remaining open to the corrective nature of the former.

But before we get to the nitty-gritty of becoming guilt-free, let's touch on how this guilt came to be and why it finds such easy access into the lives of so many moms.

How Did We Get Here?

Guilt is impartial. It affects females and males alike. Yet, I found it quite interesting that moms are more disposed to this type of parental guilt than dads. It should come as no surprise, really, seeing that society has conditioned women since girlhood to become moms someday.

~

If I were to poll a group of women, I'm sure many would be familiar with playing some version of "house" as youngsters: the game where you pretended to be an adult running a household with your children, which were usually dolls or younger siblings. Your "babies" were quite cooperative, always heeding your every wish. You had the ideal job, and some even opted for a handsome imaginary spouse – mine was either Michael Jackson or his brother Marlon depending on how the coin flip landed between my cousin and me.

Everything was simple and carefree then. We were unaware that, during those times of make-believe, a picture of what parenting was all about and the types of parent we would someday become were beginning to form subconsciously. For some of us, this was the starting point of understanding parenthood, even in the minutest way. What we lacked was the cognizance to anticipate how very different real life would be.

As we matured and started families of our own, our experiences proved to be markedly different from those fanciful ideas of parenting we held as children. We soon realized, among other things, that, unlike our dolls, real babies usually don't remain asleep until we're ready for them to awaken, and neither does our days with them always go as planned. Thus, our misconceptions showed themselves to be just that: concepts that missed the mark. Still, even though our ideal scenarios turned out to be flawed, we didn't fully part ways with the flawless pictures we'd envisioned. Instead, we held on to portions of them somewhere in our psyches, determined to make them our realities even if that meant faking it until we made it happen.

~

Although our initial understanding of parenting may have been somewhat skewed, there was one aspect we would have been wise to retain. Back then, we didn't need to consult with the other little moms as to whether we were making the best decisions for our baby. We possessed confidence in our mothering skills. We trusted ourselves. Trusting our ability to be a great mother for our children is one of the essential qualities needed to become free from mommy guilt. Doing so lessens the effect the external and internal noise has on us.

This self-trust was an innate characteristic we each possessed that has become impaired over time by the incessant messages pulling us this way and that. And as each distraction shifts our attention, it chips away at our confidence as moms while strengthening guilt's stronghold.

~

But this is only the starting point of our tussle with mommy guilt. Other factors have not only contributed to its development, but also perpetuate it in our lives.

The good news is there's hope for preventing future bouts. However, if we are to resist it moving forward, we must not only free ourselves from negative feelings and thoughts that encourage it but also become aware of the environments and unsuspected behaviors we participate in that cause it to thrive.

3

The Many Faces of Mommy Guilt

Societal Demands, Expectations, and Opinions

Never have our lives been so scrutinized as in the present time. No one, including moms, is spared from this appraisal, which has intensified since the time I first became a parent. As a matter of fact, moms have become favored targets.

It begins the moment the pregnancy is announced – "Where's the baby bump?" – and throughout the pregnancy – "How much weight has she put on?"

After the baby is born, we hear:

> *"Oh, you didn't have a natural delivery?"*
>
> *"You're back to work already?!"*
>
> *"You* are *pureeing your baby's food, right?"*

Then it's on to "How long will it take her to lose all that doggone weight?!" We're allowed to carry a baby for nine months, so long as the extra pounds are shed nine days (or less) after giving birth. All these questions are accompanied by slight looks of judgment, of course. And this is only the tip of the iceberg.

~

Sadly, this appraisal doesn't stop with us moms. Early on, our children are pulled into the assessment as well:

> *"Where are the pictures?"*
>
> *"How cute is she?"*
>
> *"What designer clothing are they wearing?"*
>
> *"Is he reading yet?"* (Mind you, this is before kindergarten!)
>
> *"Did your child make the honor roll?"*
>
> *"Which activities do they participate in?"*
>
> *"Which elite school did they get accepted into?"*

On and on, this scrutiny continues through literally every parenting phase.

~

We're pressured to be all (wife, mother, career woman, friend); do it all (work, parent, care for everyone); and have it all (physical looks, physique, fashion, material possessions). These messages come through a myriad of sources: from the big screen to the music industry, from your workplace to your neighborhood, from social media to magazines, from the local PTA to conversations with family and friends. They're almost impossible to escape.

Society makes a compelling case for maintaining a socially acceptable image. And, because we are strongly disposed to take our cues from the world around us, many of us to go to great lengths to try and fulfill the unreasonably tall order to be, do, and have it all, even if doing so leaves us mentally, financially, and spiritually bankrupt in the process. This eventually leads to mounting guilt when you're no longer able to live up to those societal expectations, especially if you're a new mom.

~

The reality is that the societal benchmark is everchanging and must be seen and resisted for what it is: an illusion. Because, regardless of what the popular song proclaims, you are not "every woman" – at least, not all at once or in every season of your life. You have limits. We all do. It's wise to recognize them.

By granting our fickle society access to come in and impose upon us its design for how we ought to live our lives, we become trapped on the proverbial hamster's wheel, chasing the next big thing that promises to make our lives more satisfying.

While we warn our children about the dangers of putting stock in the opinions of others or acquiring the herd mentality of blindly following the lead of their peers, we often fail to take our own advice.

~

One of my favorite quotes comes from Abraham Maslow. It says, "Be independent of the good opinion of other people." In other words, remain neutral to the estimation that others have of you, even when that estimation is good. Why? Because people are capricious – their opinions change like the wind. The opinions in and of themselves aren't the problem; it's how we process them. While critical opinions can potentially affect you adversely, favorable opinions can work in an equally damaging manner. They stroke your bruised ego and fill your head with pomp, causing you to depend on those outside assessments to determine your worth.

Being independent of what others think of, expect from, or how they feel about you helps you stay in tune with the path you've discerned for yourself and your child. It also curbs the tendency to compare yourself or your children to others, which is the next area that can cause mommy guilt to rear its ugly head.

Parting Ways with Comparisons

We've all heard (and probably given) the sage advice of "Don't be like everyone else" or "Be yourself." And why do we give such advice? Because, whether consciously or unconsciously, we understand the importance of maintaining our individuality if we are to experience fully the life we're meant to live. Yet, even with that awareness, we can find ourselves peeking over the fence at our neighbors' seemingly greener grass wishing ours was as plush as theirs.

Comparing ourselves to others isn't new. It's something we've done since we were children. There has been a surge in moms comparing their parenting abilities to other moms. But these days it isn't only about maintaining your reputation, but also that of your children, which ups the ante considerably. If you thought making yourself look good to others was important, making sure your child has it all together is an entirely different beast.

~

A while back, I overheard a mom having a conversation with her daughter, comparing her to another girl on her dance team. She said to her young daughter, "Why can't you look more like that other girl!? She's beautiful.

When you dance, make your face look like hers." The girl she was referring to happened to be the stand-out dancer on the team, attracting the attention of all of the dance instructors and chosen as the lead for most routines, which was obviously what the mom wanted for her daughter.

After recovering from hearing the mom's bizarre request, I attentively observed, curious to see how the little girl would respond. I watched as she returned to the dance floor, contorting her face in the most uncomfortable ways, trying to accommodate her mother's wish. I also saw a noticeable change in her countenance when she seemingly had a moment of revelation. Her eyes widened as she walked back over to her mom and excitedly stated, "Mommy, I'm not able to make my face look like hers because I don't have her face." muting her mom. She then returned to the floor and continued dancing.

I can't tell you how elated I was to see that the girl not only understood but voiced that she couldn't be anyone other than herself. And while her mom might not have been okay with that, she was.

~

Maybe you've never gone to the extremes of the story above. But have you ever found yourself asking your child to do something that would make *you* happy and bring about the results *you* were hoping for – never considering whether or not it was outside their current capacity? I have. It turns out that very incident helped me realize I had been comparing my girls to other girls who displayed qualities I wished they possessed – qualities such as being more outspoken, outgoing, or risk-taking. I was projecting onto them what I desired to see in myself.

Instead of allowing those qualities to develop naturally, if at all, I attempted to force the situation. Doing so not only caused me to ignore the anxiety this created as they struggled to do what was outside of their natural inclinations, but also caused me to disregard and disrespect the essence of who they were while teaching them to do the same.

~

Comparisons are made to determine similarities and differences between two or more things with the goal of revealing commonalities or deficiencies. When you compare your child or yourself to another, you are doing the same thing. The usual aim of this assessment is for you to feel better about yourself or your situation – whether that's done by reveling in your advantage or in the disadvantage of the other person.

Comparing in this way is damaging. It causes you to align yourself with the societal belief that you and/or your children are inadequate and need to be more. This is a lie! Just as a rosebud comes equipped with all it needs to bloom into a beautiful, mature rose, you and your child arrive here with everything you need to develop into the people you are meant to become. The choice of whether you'll accept and work with the cards you're dealt, however, is left to you.

~

Giving in to the lure of comparing compounds the guilt you experience, especially when you or your children don't seemingly measure up. It suggests that you've failed in some way. Doing so takes your focus off of all that you have and should be grateful for and places it on what you feel you lack, stirring up discontentment as you desire to be the one causing the envy instead of the one feeling it.

~

Comparing rarely shows up solo in our lives. It usually has a close acquaintance that rides shotgun, which happens to be our next mommy-guilt behavior to highlight. Comparison's cousin: competition.

Anything You Can Do I Can Do Better —Competitiveness

The topic of comparing gives us the perfect segue into the subject of competition, seeing that they both feed off of the same anxious energy. While comparing is an attempt to establish equality with or superiority over someone, the arena of competition is where you set out to prove your ranking.

~

Growing up, it seemed to me that competing was mainly reserved for areas such as sports, politics, and business. Nowadays, it permeates much of our lives. Competition is prevalent within families, friendships, between neighbors, and in the workplace. It's noticeable in our education system, evident in the fierceness of sports fans, and observed in the abundance of competitive reality shows on television.

If we're not trying to decide who's the "biggest loser," we're engaged in "cupcake wars," examining "who wore it best," and, while we're at it, determining if we're living better than someone else by asking to take a peek inside their "crib."

We've added parenting to the long list of things we approach competitively, going out of our way to ensure we and our children maintain the advantage.

~

I participated in this behavior as well, which came rather easily, seeing I had always enjoyed a good challenge. I happened to be my biggest competitor: demanding nothing short of excellence from whatever I put my hands to. I often pushed beyond my limits as I strived to outdo my last accomplishment, despising the waste of time or energy on any project I worked on that didn't produce tangible or significant results. I had a "do it big or don't do it at all" philosophy. While this way of being might work for others, it wasn't for me. The weight of such high expectations just about did me in. Although I continue to aim for excellence, I've since changed my attitude to a more relaxed "do my absolute best and rest" frame of mind.

For some time, my propensity to compete remained in check, to the point where I thought I had it under control. But, apparently, it only lay dormant, awaiting the opportune time to resurface. That time presented itself when I resigned from my government career to pursue my own business and be at home with my family.

This career change freed me to spend time volunteering at my girls' elementary and middle schools – something that I hadn't been able to do previously – which also increased the time I spent with other school moms. The majority of these interactions were pleasant, with the exception of a few that were . . . let's say, interesting. I was brought face to face with many moms, including those who thought they ruled the school (I often pictured them in pink satin jackets with black lettering on the back), as well as those who turned just about everything into a contest.

~

Head classroom mom, team mom, and chaperone selections for field trips were fiercely sought to the point where some moms resorted to flattering teachers and coaches as a way to guarantee their appointment. The desire to be known as the parent who came up with the best ideas for events or who brought the coolest gadgets to classroom parties was evident, as was wanting to be recognized for doing the most during fundraisers.

Common were comments aimed at making those within earshot aware of their child's latest accomplishment, as were disingenuous inquiries about whose class your child was in as a lead-in to announce their child was in "Mrs. So-and-so's" advanced learning class.

~

Observing this nonsense was rather entertaining initially. It even became the comedic topic of conversations I had with family and friends. There came a point, however, as this jockeying continued, when thoughts of concern replaced my laughter. Would my girls miss out on opportunities or have their abilities overlooked as a result of this posturing, especially if I didn't play along? As I fed off of this aggressive energy, my competitive juices were roused and, eventually, revived. Before long, I entered the fray. Only instead of cozying up to teachers and coaches, I began pushing my girls to perform – the same way I once tirelessly pushed myself.

Areas that I already considered priorities shifted into overdrive. I ensured my girls remained at the top of their classes by having them regularly read to secure their spots in the "Level A" reading group. I saw to it that they maintained a certain GPA to guarantee they would be invited to join high-level academic groups. I prepped Justyce extensively to secure her spot on the spelling bee team and trained Jaicie to become a top contender on her cross-country and track teams.

This senseless conduct continued for just shy of two years, during which time my family became fatigued by it all. As did I. I watched as weariness replaced the enjoyment my girls had once displayed for school and activities. Through it all, I learned that my girls hadn't inherited my competitive spirit, and that I was out of control. For them, it wasn't always about "winning" or "being the best," as I often urged.

Accepting that they wanted to learn and enjoy activities with their friends without the added pressure of feeling the need to please me meant that any guilt associated with having inadequately prepared them for one challenge or another faded from my mind. It was okay if they didn't always excel academically or bring home the blue ribbon. Instead, I encouraged them to do their absolute best and control the only thing they could – themselves – by being prepared for opportunities whenever they were presented and trust God with the outcome.[1] If they obtained the prize, great, if not, it wasn't theirs to have that go-round. Seeing them learn, mature, and enjoy their young lives *care*-free became the equivalent of a blue ribbon in my eyes.

---

[1] "God" is one of the many names I use to refer to my Higher Power. I also use Lord, Holy Spirit, my Divine Source, and Maker. I understand that there are other names people use as well, such as the Universe, Divine Intelligence, Jehovah, I Am – or none at all. However, the Source of Life is bigger than any name we can ascribe. As you read further, substitute this name with what resonates with you.

Things Aren't Always What They Seem

Before moving on, I'd like to share a couple of final thoughts on comparing and competing.

~

Gone are the days when the only proof needed to believe anything was seeing it with your own eyes. Nowadays, with so many people skilled at keeping up appearances, it's somewhat irresponsible not to assess situations with a healthy dose of skepticism.

The wonder of technology floods us with information and images so rapidly at times that we're unable to process it all. The rise of social media has taken comparing and competing to a whole new level, and is now the chosen platform for showcasing our fabulous lives, amazing kids, and everything in between. It's the place where motherhood has been reduced to vacations, parties, and matching pajamas. Filtered pictures and exaggerated words mislead many, often serving as proof that we're good moms, while leaving some moms feeling guilty for not being able to do more as they compare their lives to what they see on the screen.

For a while, I was one of those fooled by this sensationalism. I often wondered how these people – some I knew, some I didn't – could be in the throes of parenting and yet live such delightful lives. And not only that but, how could I be so "off" in how I was doing life? While I barely had enough time or energy in a day to work, cook a decent meal, help my girls with homework, keep my house clean, and shower, their timelines were filled with pictures of delicious-looking homemade meals, family bike rides, volunteering at local shelters, and quick jaunts to the city – all during a workweek.

Being a Nancy Drew fan back in the day, I put to use my own sleuthing skills to get to the bottom of this by doing what I do best – investigate. I began asking some of those people what were their secrets. How the heck were they pulling it all off? As I inquired, I was surprised by the many candid responses I received. If the thought "no one's life can be this perfect all the time" has ever crossed your mind when perusing social media, you're right.

I learned from some moms that most of what they were sharing online wasn't all it appeared to be. What was omitted from many of those posts were forced smiles, meltdowns, sleepless nights, and stress.

I also came to understand that much of this showiness wasn't done to toot their own horns as much as it was to receive approval from others. It served as a way to be seen, heard, and appreciated because, during the parenting years, it's common for moms to take a back seat to their children. This behavior and the "likes" it generated equated to doing something right as a mom.

This need for constant validation is a result of the value our culture places on developing our external lives often at the expense of building up our interior lives. This imbalance reinforces inferiority and insecurity, which then keep us participating in behaviors that produce a false sense of worth such as those aforementioned, and those that follow.

SMS - Supermom Syndrome

I'm a 70s/80s girl – the eras of great TV shows and even greater music. During that time there was a popular women's fragrance named "Enjoli" which was tagged as the "8-hour perfume for the 24-hour woman." The commercial for this product presented a woman who was able to do it all and then some. She worked, cared for her children, cooked, cleaned, and still had enough energy to turn on the heat in the bedroom.

She even had her own song that went like this: "I can bring home the bacon, fry it up in a pan, and never, never, *never* let you forget you're a man. 'Cause I'm a woman! Enjoli!" On top of all that, this woman was always perfect – even when frying bacon.

~

I recall seeing this commercial and singing along to the catchy jingle with not a clue as to the meaning behind the words. I'm pretty sure other girls and women sang along as well. There was something about it all that made my twelve-year-old self think, *Wow, look at* her. *She's cool!*

Years later, as an adult, a mother, and wife, I have a very different take on what it means to be a woman. I think back to how misleading that commercial was. Although my mother's generation was this product's target customer, somewhere along the way my generation latched on to this depiction and have been successful at propagating its message, and bent on fulfilling it, ever since.

~

Fast-forward to the present day and I marvel at how the influence of this symbol is still felt today. Except now, she has transformed into an upgraded 2.0 version. She's a character of our making affectionately known as "supermom." We've all seen her: the caricature of a mom with multiple arms, at times donning the infamous red cape, makeup on point, hair intact, her happy baby in one arm, laptop in another, multitasking with the others as she successfully and effortlessly moves through her bustling day.

We've so enthusiastically adopted this idea that it has sparked a nationwide supermom syndrome. Where some moms feel the need to wear an imaginary "S" on their chest, pushing themselves, often to their breaking point, to perform seemingly grand or impossible feats. Whether it's saving the day, being everything to everyone, or killing it in their career, they're out to prove they can do it all – with a smile, and on four hours of sleep. Many mothers take great pride in being compared to this character, as it serves as a testament to their prowess. Then there's the praise they receive for their heroism, which is a much-welcomed break from the guilt inducing voices they usually entertain.

While the above is the more popular image we're used to seeing, there is a similar portrayal of a mom shown in a strikingly different light. It's one of another many-armed mom, attempting to breeze through her many tasks, yet looking quite frazzled – her hair in disarray, coffee spilling, wearing mismatched shoes, with kids refusing to cooperate. Although many moms would have you believe they've attained the former model, their reality behind closed doors is likely closer to the latter.

As attractive as the supermom model is in theory, the false sense of power that she seduces moms with and the pressure she places on moms to stay on their A-game is as mentally and physically taxing as her attainment is overrated.

~

It's no surprise that I found the supermom image enticing, seeing that its expression is akin to competing. For me, it began with making the best homemade treats for school parties – even though I hated baking. I can't tell you the relief I felt when our school district announced that only store-bought goodies would be allowed at parties. Buying a pack of store-made cupcakes or a bag of chocolate kisses was more my speed anyway. From there, it went to throwing unique birthday parties – although they stressed me to no end – to coming up with the cutest Halloween costumes and adorable Valentines treats, all while keeping tabs on my household and running a successful home-based business. I appeared to be doing it all, making everyone happy in the process, while feeling like a chicken with its head cut off.

I tried to sustain this image but knew something was off. I felt it. Eventually, I came to realize that feeling was self-betrayal. I was behaving in a way that conflicted with who I knew myself to be. While conforming to a mold shaped by others was a sure way to gain admiration, it was just as sure a way to experience the frustration of living a lie. Although I was able to suppress the discomfort successfully for a while, there came a time when I could no longer ignore it.

Don't get me wrong, I enjoyed making those memories with my girls, but I had an underlying motive behind some of my actions: proving I *could* do it all! I learned, however, that being the poster girl for something so superficial was not the path to fulfillment, but rather to further frustration.

I reconciled that I wasn't artsy, crafty, or remotely creative enough to maintain this façade – never had been and probably never would be. I concluded it was more important for me to be a person who I liked and respected, someone who remained consistently true to myself rather than merely a person who did what others deemed likable. And with that, the charade was over. The time had come for me to ditch my beloved cape, break up with my superhero alter ego, and rid myself of this guise for good.

~

While I do believe moms possess a certain "magicalness," we were never meant to be supermoms. The magical essence I'm referring to is the steadfast love a mother displays; the confident parental wisdom she exudes; and the way she mothers intently, fearlessly, and wholeheartedly. These are qualities that genuinely inspire wonder.

So, instead of attempting to be "suuupermooom" for all to see, how about focusing on being a super mom for your audience of one . . . or two or three . . . or more, depending on how many children you have. After all, their votes are the only ones that matter.

Multi-Activitying Madness

To say our culture is addicted to activity is an understatement. It's common to hear or find ourselves proclaiming how busy we are. Downtime has become a rare luxury that, if afforded, is quickly filled with something to do. Anything!

Although most any mom would take delight in a few moments of absolute nothingness, our penchant for movement along with our aversion to saying "no" to the requests of others makes experiencing such moments almost impossible. Plus, doing so would probably make us feel guilty. So, instead, we grin, bear it, and complain about it later.

The catch is, while many moms protest about being stretched thin, there is something appealing about busyness. Maybe it's the sense of productivity this constant flurry brings or the feeling of importance it implies. My guess is that we embrace it because diverting our attention elsewhere helps to quell the guilt and other issues we would otherwise have to wrestle with.

I didn't realize it at the time, but that is precisely where I had camped out – busying myself to avoid myself. My lovely, color-coded calendar, filled with one thing after the next, served as evidence of my hectivity and often included the practice of simultaneous execution, otherwise known as multitasking. And, just as with busyness, this behavior is commonly regarded as praiseworthy among moms.

~

We have inadvertently passed this need for constant stimulation on to our children, leaving them with little concept of what it means to dial down. Nowadays, our children's calendars are just as full and color-coordinated, if not more, than our own. It's gotten to the point where even the slightest lull sets off the well-known complaint – "I'm booored!" Hearing those two words fills us with angst and guilt for not keeping them entertained (especially during breaks from school), subsequently sending us scrambling to come up with something for them to do. God forbid the proverb "an idle mind is the devil's playground" – inferring a lack of activity gives way to mischievous conduct – becomes our children's fate.

We respond to their discomfort with downtime the same way we respond to our own – by inundating and overcommitting them with activities galore or *"multi-activitying"*– the child's equivalent of multi-tasking.

~

We sympathize as we witness other moms frantically cart their child from one event or activity to the next. And if they're doing this for more than one child . . . well, we know they're toast! The importance of keeping children active is valid for many reasons. The solution, however, isn't to jam-pack their schedules with activities that only fill their time, but with ones that feed their souls and eventually fuel their sense of purpose. The goal is to eliminate the elicitor of mischief (boredom) by finding activities that are gratifying to your child. It's not the quantity of activities that counts, but the quality. One activity that can hold their full attention is better than five that don't.

Roots and Wings vs. Loot and Things

During the period when I decided to dip my toe into the waters of entrepreneurship, I found myself in the presence of the founder of a thriving new company. He was delivering an inspiring speech about success. Hearing him speak was a real treat.

After sharing best practices and tricks of the trade, he went on to explain that, while material gain or financial abundance is often the gauge used to determine success, bona fide success begins with having and living according to principles, values, and a strong moral compass in every area of life.

By far the best part of the talk came toward the end when he began sharing his personal story. His frankness in detailing the many disappointments and setbacks he experienced in life and the obstacles that, rather than shielding him from, his parents allowed him to work through was encouraging and resonated with many in attendance. He explained that those events were what ultimately allowed him to develop the resilience that was evident in his life.

His closing wasn't the typical rah-rah, "go out there and knock 'em dead" type of ending either. Instead, he, a father of eight, made a simple yet attention-grabbing statement, saying, "Parents, be sure to give your children roots and wings, not only loot and things." Wow! What an unorthodox way to end a leadership and sales meeting by appealing to the parents in attendance.

~

That was the first time I'd ever heard that saying. And although the gist of what he meant was clear, those words stuck with me until I had given them proper consideration, which I did.

What can be gleaned from this thought of promoting roots and wings over loot and things? I'm glad you asked.

Loot, Things

These days, consumerism or materialism is the name of the game. Virtually everyone must have the latest and greatest of everything.

Loot and things, in this context, refer to the money and material gains parents lavish on their children.

We're made to believe that the more we have, the happier we'll be. Sure, material things can brighten our day and cheer us up when we're down, which might be why some moms who find themselves in guilt-laced episodes resort to giving things as a way to assuage those guilty feelings. And you know what? That works, but only momentarily. The guilt that lingers proves this type of guilt-giving doesn't address the underlying issues. While your child will gladly receive the goods, using them as a means to drown out the voice of guilt within yourself or to appease your child falls short as a real solution.

This quick fix doesn't come without cost. For instance, by repeatedly overindulging our children with things in exchange for the time, attention, or affection we may fail to give, are we indirectly teaching them that to be pacified with materials is acceptable? Are we sending the message that, in our eyes, time spent with them is equivalent to a pair of shoes, headphones, or a video game?

~

Like any mom, seeing my girls happy made me happy. Likewise, hearing disappointment in their voices, especially when I was the producer of it, would ignite guilt within me.

Although their sadness was genuine, it didn't take long for them to put two and two together and realize they could benefit from my guilt-riddenness. During those moments when I had to make the tough decision of choosing work or some other responsibility over being with them, both would appear before me, side by side, long faces and all, with their usual requests for cookie dough and mint chocolate chip ice cream. And just like that, off we went to Baskin-Robbins.

Over time, it occurred to me that by giving in to their requests, I was teaching them that it was okay to be manipulative toward someone who found themselves in an unfortunate position. *That* was not okay.

So, instead of my usual reaction of reaching for the car keys to run out and quench their thirst for "things," I decided to flip the script by giving them one of my famous heart-to-heart-to-heart chats, which they very much disliked. The fact that I had other tasks to attend to didn't make me a villain or translate to some wrongdoing for which I needed to compensate them for. It only meant I had a life outside of my children.

~

While loot and things have their place, they mustn't be our go-to for dealing with mommy guilt.

Finding yourself in this type of rock-and-hard-place predicament shouldn't automatically result in you shoving things your child's way to make it all better. Acknowledge their disappointment and, even if you can't make it right in their eyes, your recognition of the situation will prove to ease the upset.

Roots, Wings

Loot and things are pretty self-explanatory. But what exactly do roots and wings represent? At first thought, the function of these two might seem conflicting. Roots bind, whereas wings are used to set free. So how do these two work in harmony?

~

In nature, roots are the underground supports of a plant or tree. They are the system that provides the nourishment required for proper growth. Without a strong root system, the tree or plant will fail to yield fruit or produce any other desired result. In the same way, we provide roots for our children in the form of love, care, nurture, guidance, morals, and values to name a few. These things nourish them, keep them grounded, and provide stability for growth.

Wings are needed not only to fly but must also have the strength to keep in flight. I've had the pleasure of seeing the flight of a bald eagle on a couple of occasions. One time, in particular, I was so fascinated that I had to pull over on the side of the road to fully take it in. With its grand wingspan, it skillfully soared through the air before gracefully switching over to an effortless waltz with the wind. Breathtaking! Its wings were a source of strength that granted freedom and independence.

~

We are to help our children develop their full wingspan so that they too are capable of soaring in life. As such, we want to make sure we strengthen their wings, not clip them. A couple of ways we can do so is by empowering them with age-appropriate responsibilities and providing room to make good choices as well as learn from their mistakes. We can clip their wings by shielding them from essential life lessons that aid in their development or passing onto them our inordinate fears that cause them to doubt themselves or their decision-making abilities.

In giving them roots and wings, we establish a solid foundation of love, support, and encouragement, while at the same time, permitting the experiences necessary for them to grow and take their breathtaking flight through life.

4

Child Care

The obvious prerequisite for being troubled by mommy guilt is being a mom. As such, more than family, friends, or outsiders, our children are the source most capable of provoking the storm of guilt within us.

I'm convinced that most parents would do just about anything to ensure their children's success. Early on, we dream about who they will grow up to become and, more accurately, who we'd like to see them become. Some of us even go as far as taking matters into our own hands, steering our children down a path that we feel would be most advantageous. And I get it. Having so much of ourselves (physical attributes, personality, mannerisms) reflected in them, and considering all that we invest in them, we tend to view them as our possession. And since they're ours, shouldn't we be able to have this kind of influence and input? Nah, I don't believe so. They don't arrive here as a clean slate to do with as we wish. They come equipped with a purpose and divine intelligence of their own that's more invested in guiding them to find and fulfill that purpose than we are. We'll touch more on this in Chapter 6.

The way we view and relate to our children can either increase or reduce guilt flare-ups. The many desires and expectations we have for them, as good as they may be, can lead to our disappointment and subsequent guilt when life interrupts our plans and takes our children down a different road.

~

I'm aware that any discussion regarding how one chooses to interact with or raise their child can be a touchy one, but I feel it's one we can effectively maneuver. Before we begin, let's pinky promise to remain friends when you're done reading this section. Okay? Okay.

The Matter of Time

When I surveyed moms about what most triggered their guilt, without question, time (or the lack thereof) topped the list. Not having enough time and desiring to spend more of it with their children being the most common problem mentioned. Having once been weighed down by this trigger myself, I could relate. The guilt I experienced when such feelings emerged pained me. I mean, it literally gave me a stomachache. For a while, I reasoned that the twenty-four hours I had been given simply weren't enough. I knew that any effort to acquire more of this precious commodity would be useless. That is, until a look at how I spent my twenty-four-hour allotment proved otherwise.

~

I often think of life as a school where we enroll and are expected to complete and learn from specific course-work that's assigned to us. These courses consist of primary assignments that include caring for our well-being and the well-being of our family. In addition, there are optional extracurricular activities that we may also choose to participate in. These are secondary to our primary assignments, and qualifying for them depends on how successful we are at completing the main coursework. There's no end to what these extra activities can include: pursuing business ventures, sitting on boards or committees, optional work trips, additional outings with friends, etc. These can be tricky because the enjoyment, productivity, and even benefit they might produce make it easy to justify our participation in them.

I believe, just as in regular school, that ample time is provided for all that is assigned to us. The sense of not having enough time for any of our primary assignments might be caused by a failure to distinguish between what's primary and what's secondary. We often add more secondary commitments into our day than our personal bandwidth allows. It's these additional commitments that are usually the culprits for feeling the way we do. The more add-ons we engage in, the less time we can devote to our assignments. When this happens, you find yourself borrowing time from one of the other areas, with family often ending up with the shortest end of the stick.

Time-Devouring Distractions

There's another time-stealing practice that's just as common as the add-ons – it's the squandering of time while with your child. Huh? Yep. How many can relate to these scenarios:

You plan a day at the park with your child. While there, you run into a friend. Instead of pushing your child on the swings or waiting for him at the bottom of the slide, you find yourself catching up with said friend for just about the entire hour that you're there, all the while smiling and waving at your child as he calls out for you to "Look, Mom!"

Or, you surprise your child by picking up a DVD that she's wanted to watch with you for weeks. After dinner you put it on, it begins to play, and, less than twenty minutes into it, you pull out your phone or laptop and commence to surf the net or check work emails – periodically glancing up at the television and pretending to follow along.

These are a couple of examples from my own history book that causes me to cringe each time they're brought to mind. It was these types of incidents that got me to thinking: *Could I be spending more time with my girls than I realized, but being distracted while with them is distorting my perception of time?* Yes, that is precisely what was happening.

This revelation squashed my "lack of time" argument. Not having enough time and the misuse of time are two different things. In both instances, the time was there, but I mismanaged it. I didn't need *more* time; I just needed to make better use of my time.

~

We've lost our respect for time. With its ranking of importance having seemingly dropped below that of money and image, time is no longer regarded as valuable. Yet, it's the only thing we spend without any knowledge of how much we have remaining. We can make more money, but we can't make more time.

~

Perhaps your problem isn't an actual shortage of time either, but, instead, it's the consumption of time by the plethora of distractions vying for your attention. One way to put the guilt associated with perceived time shortage to bed is taking advantage of the times you do spend time with your children: in the morning before school, on the drive home from school, listening when they tell you that same story for the umpteenth time, during dinner, before bed, and just hanging around the house. Put down your phone, turn off the TV, power down your tablet, and when you're with them, be *with* them, and make every limited minute count.

Like any relationship, the ones we have with our children must be developed and nurtured, and time is a crucial ingredient for achieving that.

~

What's the takeaway here? Simple. Guard your time. Watch it like a hawk. If you are to avoid getting caught up in the time-snatching trap of endless distractions, you must become a fierce protector of your time.

I'll be the first to tell you it's not always easy. However, by prioritizing your life, acknowledging your limits, and keeping the first things first, you minimize the occasions where other less important things steal your time. Also, learn to say no. Stop trying to make everybody happy, because you can't. That alone can free up more time than you realize.

~

It would be naïve of me to suggest those are the only situations that engender a sense of time shortage. There are also occasions when a shortage of time isn't imagined, but factual. For instance, what about the single mom who must work long hours or a second job to keep a roof over her family's heads and food on the table? Or how about the mom who *is* attentive to her children and careful not to over-obligate herself, yet her demanding work schedule calls for regular periods when she's away from her family?

The mental tug of war between being a mom and pursuing a career is a common struggle many moms find themselves in. The challenge of wanting to provide the most fulfilling life for herself and her family, and doing so can often mean spending considerable amounts of time away from her children.

So, what's a mom to do? Conceding to the guilt certainly isn't the answer. Instead, finding ways to reduce the strain your job has on your time can ease the tension. Consider any changes, either temporary or permanent, you can make, such as scaling back by not taking on additional work assignments that have the potential to interfere with your home life. And while it might not be feasible or even desired to part ways with your job, ask yourself questions such as: How is my job impacting my family? Is this the best job for me in this season of life? Is this the best time to take that promotion?

It boils down to deciding what's best for your family. You'll find that a carefully considered decision will strengthen your resolve and silence the bouts of guilt that are sure to arise. However, be aware that, over time, the winds can shift, weakening your surety as such questions as, "What was I thinking when I made this decision?" and "Was this the right choice?" begin to cast doubt in your mind. This is when a contingency plan comes in handy. Writing down your reason for the decision you make at the moment you make it will provide something to revisit when doubt or guilt darkens your door. Reviewing it will return you to the frame of mind you initially held, reminding and reassuring you of your decision.

~

Also, when making such decisions, be sure to take into account the entire family. I emphasize "entire" because, often, career pursuits can take precedence over everything. We move ahead, often failing to consider the potential stress our decisions can cause our children. They're expected to simply adjust to our changing routines. But, just because something is right for you, doesn't make it right for everyone involved.

Roll Call – Being Present

Some time ago, I connected with a dear friend over lunch to catch up. I enjoy spending time with her because, besides being just plain cool, she's exceptionally purposeful in all that she does, be it listening, planning events, giving advice – you name it.

During our talk, and before the expression became as widely used as it is today, she said, "I'm learning to be present in every moment of my life; with myself and with my family." At the time, I didn't fully grasp what she meant, but it made me take note, so I tucked it away. It wasn't until a couple of years later – when my life had become busier than I liked, my daughters were getting older, and I felt their childhood slipping through my fingers – that the light bulb came on and I began to understand and appreciate the gift of presence.

~

Being present is synonymous with being "in the moment." It's involved, engaged, and completely attentive to what you're doing and who you're doing it with while you're doing it.

I, like so many others, had become accustomed to either routinely sleepwalking through my day or moving so fast that much of what was going on around me or within me escaped my attention. It became apparent that something had to give when, on several occasions, my girls asked if I remembered something we'd done together or something they'd told me and my answer time and again was a reluctant "no." Their long faces were enough to send my guilt meter through the roof. It came to the point where I had to stop and ask myself, *Why the heck can't I remember all of these events?* That's when it hit me: I had been with them physically during those times but had mentally checked out.

And isn't that the worse? Being with or talking to someone and noticing his or her attention is elsewhere. It reminds me of being in my seventh-grade band. My teacher, Mr. Franklin, often became utterly annoyed as he tried to teach a piece of music only to be muffled by a bunch of chattering pre-teens preoccupied with separate conversations. He responded by tapping (or, more accurately, banging) his baton on his stand, raising his hands above his head, rapidly fidgeting his fingers, and shouting, *"Can I have your undivided attention please!?"* We all thought it was the funniest sight. Even thinking about it now makes me chuckle. But it got our attention every time.

Our children are asking the same of us. Their "bang on the stand" may play out a bit differently, however. It can show itself in many ways, such as them giving us the silent treatment, acting out of character, or rebelling. This is their cry for our undivided attention because, to them, attention received for unpleasant behavior is still attention.

~

I can't honestly say that I was completely attentive from that moment on, but I became more aware of the times that I wasn't. During this period of waking up in life, I made a point to be an active participant when with my girls instead of just passively present. I found that when I gave them my undivided attention, they soaked it up and became more engaged and expressive. But my girls weren't the only ones who benefited. I noticed how I appreciated the courtesy of someone's undivided attention as well and felt slighted when I didn't receive it. This helped me understand how my girls might have interpreted my past inattentiveness as indifference.

Not only did reining in my focus help me remember our times together, slowing my pace enabled me to become more aware and also seemed to magically add more time to my days. Although I wasn't able to recover the time I felt I'd misspent, I was able to get the most out of our time together moving forward.

~

It's been said that your time is the most valuable resource you can give someone. There's truth to that. However, what's of the highest value is giving another your time together with your full attention, or being present. That type of connection is what forms a bond with your child where you're able to get into their heart space and begin deciphering who they truly are.

Give your children your undivided attention while they desire it. Before long, their attention will become fixed on other things, and you'll find yourself craving then, what they want now.

This practice of being present proves beneficial in other areas as well. Namely, when it comes to making decisions concerning your children, and during their rapidly changing developmental stages.

Being Present in Decision Making

I've experienced regret for decisions I made for my girls that led to them taking part in things that didn't end well. This regret was followed by guilt for being the one who approved of their participation. This tore at me emotionally and made me question my own parental decision-making abilities for a while.

Over time, I began to understand that there would be some misfortunes my girls would experience simply because it's a part of the growth and developmental plan necessary for them. Knowing I wouldn't be aware of those unfavorable outcomes on the front end made being attentive and fully present when making all decisions concerning them essential. This wasn't a way to absolve myself from decisions I made on their behalf that went amiss. It was recognizing and surrendering to the fact that even when doing all that I could to seek guidance for parenting my girls and making the best decisions with the information I had, some things would still be out of my control.

From decisions as seemingly inconsequential as allowing them to ride their bikes to the local store or going to see a movie with friends, to those more considerable such as allowing them to stay overnight at a family member or friend's house or going away for a weekend camp – all received equal and careful consideration.

~

Giving this level of attention to the decisions I made for my girls was a practice I started after experiencing the fallout of failing to heed subtle hunches I periodically received in decision-making moments. This revealed that being fully present when making decisions for my children also required that I became fully present with what was taking place inside of me as well.

I'm sure you can attest to instances where you didn't follow your gut instinct, only to realize that the intuitive insight you received was spot-on.

This brings to mind an incident that took place during my pre-mom days. My niece (who is like a daughter to me) received an invitation to a birthday party. She'd just started a new elementary school and made a few friends who neither my sister or I had yet gotten to know. For this reason, I had some reservations regarding her attendance and expressed my concern. However, after her constant pleading with my sister, she was allowed to go.

My sister dropped her off and, later that evening, while out running errands, I passed the restaurant where the party was being held. As I drove by, I experienced an urge to pop in and see how things were going. However, since the girl who invited her was considered a friend, I convinced myself that I was over-reacting. Besides, knowing the stink-eye my niece would have delivered had I showed my face, I continued with my plans. I mean, what could go wrong?

Later that night, when she arrived home, I saw the anguish on her face before she or my sister spoke a word. It turned out that the party was a disaster from the start. The "friend" who had invited her ignored and excluded her and a couple of other girls the entire night, making her time there less than festive. This incident bothered me for days and introduced the importance of listening to the Still Small Voice within, that guides and leads beyond obvious perception.

~

This level of attentiveness would only increase when it came to my own children. For instance, when Jaicie was much younger and visiting a neighbor's house, she asked if she could play in their pool. Considering she was still learning how to swim, I told both her and my neighbor that she could play in the yard but not in the pool. Later that day, I needed to run to the store, so I walked over to get her. My neighbor assured me, "She can stay until you get back. The girls are having fun. It's fine." I immediately felt a sense of caution but, with the store being nearby and knowing I would be gone for only a short while, I overrode my intuition and allowed her to stay.

Upon returning, I went to pick her up and what did I behold – my daughter, in full swim attire, frolicking in the pool with her friend, as happy as a jaybird – until she saw me. I, on the other hand, was fuming. Not only had Jaicie ignored my instructions, so had my neighbor, who, might I add, was barely watching them.

As we walked home, and throughout the night, all kinds of dreadful thoughts of how disastrous that incident could have turned out ran through my mind. Although Jaicie was fine, I didn't take the happy ending for granted. I knew that what I'd sensed earlier was communication of a different kind, and to ignore any of its future warnings could result in very different outcomes. It wasn't something I was willing to gamble with, which was enough for me to vow to never again override that guidance.

In case you're wondering, I did address the situation with my neighbor after my blood had stopped boiling, and when little ears were no longer present.

~

These incidents and others like them were what I cut my teeth on when learning to be sensitive to the internal guidance that I knew to be of a higher origin. They taught me not to dismiss what I sensed concerning decisions for my girls even when it appeared illogical on the surface or meant ruffling feathers – be they the feather of my girls or other people.

~

Now, the internal voice that I referred to above isn't to be confused with the bruised, egoic inner mean girl we discussed earlier. This voice is what I've come to know as God's voice within me. While both voices reside within each of us simultaneously, one is benevolent and the other brutish, one helpful and the other harsh, one is patient and the other often anxious. Loudening the one while drowning out the other can prove to be of great value.

Although learning to work with this inner guide requires practice, it doesn't have to be a long, drawn-out process. Begin by taking a moment to ask for guidance or give your attention to what needs to be addressed and pay attention to how you feel about it. I like to refer to this direction as my guidance system, and I've come to trust the inward impressions I receive. On a much simpler level, I compare it to the red light, yellow light, and green light traffic signal system that I'm sure most are familiar with. It goes a little something like this:

Red (stop/no) – This is an uneasy sensation that arrests your attention. A feeling similar to blinking warning lights going off inside of you. And, while you might not perceive any imminent danger, heeding this warning can be a literal lifesaver.

Yellow (slow/proceed with caution) – This feels like indecisiveness or hesitation. You want to give the go-ahead but something within you won't allow it. Instead, further evaluation is necessary.

Green (all clear/yes) – Feels like silence, calm, or stillness, giving you the okay to proceed.

As you become familiar with this safe inner language, it will become a reliable personal advisor. Taking the few moments necessary to evaluate each situation will be something you'll thank yourself for later.

Ever-Changing Times

Parenting is far from a walk in the park. Our children's journeys through the many phases of life can bring a mix of joys and pains. While we all experience occasions when we would like the clock to slow down, what about those phases where us moms wish time would accelerate a bit?

You know, those stages when they're constantly nursing as babies or have yet to sleep through the night, causing us to look forward to when they become toddlers. Then, as toddlers, when they begin walking and getting into everything, we eagerly await the day they'll start school. School age finally arrives and all of the busyness it brings makes us in desperate need of a break. On and on this cycle continues until high school graduation day looms on the horizon, revealing the brevity of the time it took to arrive there. It's then that we realize that this parenting adventure was designed to be experienced at a marathon pace instead of the sprint we often make it out to be.

This particular attitude can be attributed to mere exhaustion and a touch of frustration, both of which are understandable. In my case, however, there were times when something more was going on. The impatience I sometimes felt toward my children reflected the impatience, frustration, and dissatisfaction I had with myself. The parts of their development that I wanted to hurry through or wished I could skip over mirrored areas within myself that I didn't want to deal with.

Becoming a mom didn't automatically make me an expert at it; I had a lot to learn. One lesson it taught me was that being my children's authority figure didn't exempt me from learning from them. They are just as much my teachers as I am theirs. Those times of discontent weren't to be hastened. Instead, they were opportunities for my growth if only I humbled myself and learned from the teachers those lessons were coming through – my children. As they matured through the different stages, I wasn't only to be a witness of that growth, but being present during those times helped me to grow and evolve as a mom and woman as well.

~

Time flies enough on its own without our attempt to hurry it along. And who's to say we'll make it to the future time we're racing towards? The only time promised is the present. Not hours, days, months, or years. Only right now. As you anticipate what's to come, slow down enough to savor what's right in front of you.

Rethinking Ordinary

There isn't a parent I know who aspires for their children to be "ordinary." On the contrary, we desire for them to stand out, make their mark on the world, and accomplish big things in life. As noble as those desires are, they can feed directly into the guilt we experience as moms when those things don't happen as we hope. This is when the tape in our mind labeled "shoulda, woulda, coulda" begins to play, questioning where we went wrong and rehearsing what we might have done differently.

The surge of messages urging us all to be "extraordinary" or "great" fuels this pursuit. Because, in a day when grand displays of ability are golden, the thought of your child being "ordinary" isn't good enough. But what if being ordinary isn't as tragic as some people have made it out to be?

~

I used to spend time daydreaming about the amazing things my girls would someday accomplish. Who hasn't at some point? Did I have the next Mozart under my roof, or was I grooming the next Einstein? This fantasy appeared to be taking shape when, one day, while I was picking up Jaicie from elementary school, her music teacher stopped me as I was exiting the building.

She asked if Jaicie had ever played the piano. "No," I replied, "why do you ask?" With excited voice and eyes, she explained how some of the students dabbled around on her piano, and she was impressed that Jaicie played a particular piece perfectly on the first try. But you want to know what *I* heard: "*Mrs. Reed, you have a prodigy on your hands.*" To which I responded with a calm "*Reeeally?!*" as I inwardly jumped for joy. And with that, I was off to the races. I hired a piano instructor, bought a keyboard, bench, lesson books – the works. All the while, thinking this could be the start of something big because, hey, you never know. And, by the way, my reaction was similar when a couple of her track coaches told me they saw "real potential" in her.

~

The driving force behind this obsession with extraordinariness or greatness in our children isn't usually their desire; it's often our bruised ego seeking approval vicariously through our children. A bruised ego is the source of misery and dissatisfaction with self. It convinces us that we're lacking and the only way to prove our worth is by making a name for ourselves. The excessive amount of attention placed on attaining the status of extraordinary or great plays right into this deception.

My rule of thumb when dealing with my bruised ego is to believe the opposite of what it tells me, which, in most cases, is the truth. So it is in this case. There is nothing that we lack, including the extraordinariness we're in search of. We're only defining it incorrectly, and looking for it in the wrong place. It isn't something that requires striving to attain. It's something we inherently are. And, interestingly enough, the vehicle through which our "extra" quality is expressed is our ordinary self.

Unfortunately, possessing remarkable talent, accomplishing astounding achievements, acquiring abundant fame, or amassing profuse fortune has become the criteria for measuring extraordinariness or greatness. When these measures aren't achieved, we continue seeking external sources to fill the perceived void. What isn't understood is that the types of "extraordinary" most people strive for is worked into the agreement or contract of an individual's life and, therefore, cannot be manufactured. In other words, it's agreed upon before one's arrival here, making it divinely appointed. If working hard to make such things happen was the only requirement, anyone who desired that level of success would have a sure path to it – but that's not the case.

While remaining active in our world is a necessary and undeniable part of life, who we are isn't defined by what we do. Genuine extraordinariness isn't primarily found in *doing* external deeds or obtaining possessions. It's found in *being*. What do I mean by "being?"

Similar to how your fingerprints distinguish you from the other nearly eight billion people on earth, you have an internal imprint that's exclusively yours. This inner well, abundant with rich resources (courage, talents, gifts, ideas, solutions), is specific to you. This is what I call your "extra" – the unique outward expression of who you are at your core. While others can mimic things that you do, there isn't another individual with your exact mind, abilities, viewpoint, passion, experiences, etc., who can be you.

Accessing your well and all its richness requires intentionally slowing down frequently enough to do so. Stilling your thoughts and actions can do this. Living in a way that draws from that inner well – by connecting to, identifying with, and genuinely expressing yourself – make for a fulfilled life. This is "being." But instead of tapping into this internal treasure house by embracing our uniqueness, we're conditioned to imitate what we see in others. Yet, it is from this space of "being" that your "extra" is revealed.

~

The truth is, we're all "ordinary" people living out our unique human experience. We may not possess any outwardly special or noteworthy ability, yet we all have a definite purpose. And while we may never end up on a talk show, set world records, or have our purpose acknowledged by, appeal to, or register one iota on the radar of the masses, it has great significance in the grand scheme of things.

The thought of your child possessing a rare talent or accomplishing some great feat is fun to imagine. And if you observe unusual gifts or notable talents in your child then by all means cultivate them. At the same time, we mustn't run ahead with our own self-serving, subjective overestimations of our child, misguiding them in the process. Allow your child to be who they are ordinarily and, from that space, their "extra" will shine through.

~

Update: Turns out, Jaicie lost interest in track, and her piano ability never matched Mozart's. However, her skills at tickling the ivories opened a few doors to some pretty incredible opportunities.

Decoding Their Genius

So, is there a way to determine the areas in which your child will best flourish or whether he or she does possess any specific gifts? While we might not receive all of the intricate details, I believe we, as moms, can catch glimpses of the sparks within our children that, when ignited, causes them to come alive and thrive.

These hints can include interests that your child pursues without you needing to prompt them, and are often accompanied by a heightened degree of enthusiasm. They can also be a bit subtler, showing in the way your child processes thoughts, as well as in their sensitivities or dispositions.

Realizing that these hints don't show up on a specific timetable makes being observant and embracing a go-with-the-flow attitude a necessity. This knowledge won't eliminate trial and error, but it will reduce the myriad of options that pressure you to try and fit your square-peg child into society's round hole.

Then there are times when we desire our children to follow in our footsteps, which can actually smother the emergence of their genius. Holding strong desires for them to attend our alma mater, continue in the family business or practiced profession, or participate in activities we once loved, have a way of influencing the way we guide our children. It can also block our ability to separate the clues we receive about them from those desires we hold for them. Life is gracious and proficient at course-correcting, however, and will eventually show us the way.

~

I recall how I once tried to push ahead with my plan for Jaicie: from a very early age, she began favoring her left hand. I, however, with my "mother knows best" attitude, was set on her being right-handed, like me. I regularly attempted to overrule her preference by placing her sippy cup, spoon, crayons, and toys in her right hand. Still, no matter how much I tried to sway her from preferring her left hand, she continued to gravitate toward it. I eventually gave in and accepted the fact that my selfish desire was no match for her unconditioned nature that fought for what it knew was right.

Of course, this example isn't as weighty as deciphering the path your child should take; still, it shows how we can attempt to fill in the blanks of our children's lives with our own conclusions. With so much about their lives out of our control, we must hold loosely to the dreams we have for them, allowing the divine plan to unfurl.

More Guidance, Less Control

I received a call from a good friend of mine needing advice concerning her ten-year-old daughter, Maury. She was the new kid at her school trying to integrate into her new environment and befriend some classmates who gave my friend reservations. While Maury was still into dolls and friendship bracelets, these new girls' attention was on clothes, nails, boys, and such.

The main issue my friend contended with, however, swirled around Maury's hair. All of the girls wore their hair straight, whereas she wore her naturally curly locks pulled back in a ponytail. To give a little backstory, styling her hair that way would cause it to puff up like a tumbleweed by midday, setting off a wave of laughs and jokes from the other girls, which ultimately ended in embarrassment for Maury.

Not wanting to stand out or draw negative attention to herself, she asked if she could go to the salon to have her hair straightened. My friend explained how she'd dismissed the idea because "that's not how *we* wear our hair." She continued to share that, as a young girl, she'd never visited the salon to have her hair styled because her mom wouldn't allow it. She would wet her hair and put it in a ponytail, the same way she currently styled Maury's. "That's how *we* do it," she said. I paused and asked, "*We*" . . . or *you*? Does her experience have to be what you experienced?" This question resulted in silence.

Instead of her knee-jerk reaction, I suggested she reach back to her ten-year-old self and look at it from her daughter's current point of view. To consider how she would have liked her mother to respond if she, at that age, found herself in a similar humiliating situation day in and day out.

Looking at it from that perspective, my friend and her daughter were able to come to a compromise. She agreed to allow Maury to have her hair straightened at the salon occasionally and, in between visits, she found a way to minimize her ponytail puff. It required the effort of finding the time to go to the salon and searching for the right hair products, but it resulted in a happy girl, a happy mom, and happy hair.

~

Often, when making decisions concerning our children, we can find ourselves referencing the way we did things back in the day, with our rationale being, "If it was good enough for me, it's good enough for them." This stance is understandable since our past experiences are pretty convincing. After all, we turned out okay.

If we were to take an honest look, however, we'd see how some of the guidance we give our children teeters on the verge of being – dare I say it – controlling. Not the parental control that's necessary to keep them safe and run an orderly household, but the kind of control that's motivated by an attempt to avoid anything that thrusts us out of our comfort zones.

~

We often fear what we cannot control. Maintaining control of a situation gives a sense of being able to manage the outcome as well. It's a mechanism to keep our lives flowing in predictable patterns. Our penchant for sticking with what's familiar in some ways acts as risk management, leaving as little room as possible for our children's choices to disturb our comfort.

Having experienced similar situations and knowing what to expect can definitely help us guide our children around life's landmines. That guidance, however, must come from wanting to properly steer them and not our attempt to mitigate any disquiet their decisions may cause us. Discomfort and heartache come with the gift of parenthood, and no amount of manipulation will prevent it. To say it another way, parenting devoid of some degree of discomfort is not true parenting.

~

As I stated, some control is necessary. Boundaries ought to be drawn and rules set and observed by your children. The controlling behavior I'm referring to is when parental authority is exercised in a way to achieve an outcome more advantageous to you than to your child. The privilege of parenthood isn't given to shape our children into miniature versions of ourselves, but to take part in the unmasking of their true identity.

Room to Grow

I had a lovely childhood growing up with my mom and two older sisters. Summer was always my favorite season. The long days were mostly spent outdoors playing hopscotch, jumping rope, or skipping on the curb. Back then, it was safe to roam around the neighborhood. Riding my bike to the corner store for penny candy or over to one of my many friends' homes to play were daily routines.

I loved the amount of freedom I had. My mom never smothered me. She allowed me to explore and encouraged me to try new things. She wasn't one to shy away from voicing her recommendations for me, yet she never burdened me with expectations of fulfilling her desires for me. Although fairly lenient, she knew when and how to lay down the law. When I made mistakes, she was never one to say, "I told you so," being less concerned about proving she was right and more interested in the lessons I learned from those mistakes. Lessons that made me a rather quick learner, as I didn't particularly enjoy the sting those experiences often produced.

~

When I became a mom, I didn't quite follow suit. My naturally careful disposition, combined with seeing the world through my adult eyes, caused me to parent with heightened caution. I was determined to preserve my girls' innocence for as long as possible. The way I constantly guarded them, you would've thought I played center for the NBA, swatting away the bad and letting in only what I determined was good, be it TV shows, music, or friends.

I will never forget the day Justyce, at a very young age, came home from school singing a tune I considered inappropriate. The song didn't contain any expletives or suggestive language; it was simply something I wasn't ready for her to be exposed to, but exposed she had been. As she sang her little heart out, I stood, nearly hyperventilating, feeling as if I had been violated in some way. *After all I've done to keep her from this very thing; how did this happen!?* was my thought.

That's when it became clear that, unless I planned on cloning myself so I could be with my girls 24/7, there was no possible way to insulate them against all the negative influences, actual or perceived, that bombarded them. The bubble I had carefully placed them in was no longer practical. It was actually becoming a handicap, as life threatened to put a pin to it. Not only that but, as Jaicie and Justyce grew, they began showing signs of wanting out. Signs that I sometimes failed to see. While it was my responsibility to protect them, I was equally responsible for preparing them for the reality they encountered daily. This required teaching and coaching, not only guarding. I knew that, no matter how much I wanted to keep with this living arrangement, it was time to vacate the bubble and initiate a change in my approach.

During this approach-adjusting period, discerning at what point my children were ready to move up the next rung of exposure became a concern, as I didn't want them to advance prematurely. I began by placing myself in my girls' shoes to better understand them and obtain perspective through their eyes. This required maintaining a nimble mind, as I had to regularly shift between the mindset of a child, adolescent, and teenager depending on which daughter I was dealing with at the time. It turned out to be an eye-opening time that led me down some unexpected paths, with surprising discoveries.

Winds of Change

It's clichéd, I know, but our children really do grow up fast. We are often caught off guard by the swiftness of their maturation, so much so that we find ourselves holding back tears as we ask, "Where did the time go?" Although it might seem as if they leap from one stage to the next overnight, we know that's not quite the case. Gradual changes are taking place along the way. Some are so routine that we disregard them. Others are so subtle that we tend to overlook their significance when, all the while, they're precursors to other momentous changes at work.

As crazy as it might sound, one such overlooked occurrence is the shift from being referred to as "mommy" to being called "mom" or "ma," as my girls now call me.

~

When our children are young, we're affectionately known as "mommy." Hearing your children refer to you as such can generate feelings of endearment – or irritation, depending on the day. In your young child's eyes, "mommy" knows everything. She can do no wrong. This is a time when we impart to our children all that we know, and they pretty much mirror the values and beliefs we hold.

There comes a time, however, as your children grow and begin to experience the world around them, when their understanding of life begins to develop. It's during this time, when they are beginning to exercise their individuality and form their own opinions, when you start to become "mom." I say "start" because a vacillation between being "mommy" and "mom" is sure to happen as they test out this new vernacular. The arrival of this change is an inkling that their minds are expanding and they desire to be a bit more independent. Now, granted, at times, this change is just that – a shift in reference and nothing more. However, there are times when this title change can suggest more.

Another way this desire for more independence can manifest is in your children's piqued curiosity about life and the world around them. This is usually coupled with a multitude of "why" questions. They may even begin to notice and question hypocrisies they encounter – particularly in the adults in their life. And, being the inquiring creatures that they are, they might start questioning your personal views or actions. Ouch!

The first few times you're met with this foreign behavior it might cause a shock to your system. As hard as it might be, allow the inquiry, so long as it's done respectfully. Try to resist the temptation to quench their expression by hushing them. Call to mind the times you encouraged them to speak up for themselves or use their voice. Refuse to become offended now that you're on the receiving end of that newly found voice. They are merely testing out their God-given and, often, mom-encouraged faculties of reasoning, inquiry, and plain ol' common sense. Instead, use it as a time to listen, learn, and teach.

~

Those changes can all take place before arriving at the pivotal early-adolescent years. This is a time when your child is working through the many changes within and challenges around them. At the same time, many moms are coming to grips with the fact that their babies are babies no more. On top of that, this time often includes other transitions occurring within the family, making this already fragile period even more delicate. Whether you find yourself tending to other family members, fully engaged in your demanding career, or still figuring out life for yourself, you mustn't neglect to help your teen navigate through this very sensitive and, at times, stressful period in theirs.

~

Throughout the many phases of your child's life, the guilt gauge can wax in intensity. The teen years, however, is usually when we expect things to go into overdrive. Why? Because just as we've bought into the idea that their twos are going to be terrible, we brace ourselves as we enter the teenage years, expecting all hell to break loose. Consequently, we come to this stage ready to fight fire with fire – with that fire often manifesting in the form of words.

Miscommunication can increase as most parents and teens tend to speak different languages during this stage. This often leads to misunderstandings that escalate to rash speech, hurt feelings, regret, and yes, guilt. Will there be challenges? Heck yeah! But we can dodge a four-alarm fire by maintaining control of our fire starter – our tongue.

One way to thwart this potential firestorm is to smother it. That's right, put a lid on it. Effective communication is the foundation of any good relationship, and our relationship with our children is no different. Trying to converse with someone you've upset or you're angry at will likely cause further friction, making the timing of communication crucial. I know . . . we like to set things straight and let them know the deal.

But sometimes allowing the smoke to clear and tension to wane by thinking through our thoughts is the best approach.

This communication goes beyond merely resolving disputes. It extends into assuring them that their voice matters. An area teens wish their moms (and dads) better understood is they desire to be heard just as much as we adults do. They want the freedom to express themselves without being interrupted mid-sentence or silenced before their thoughts are fully formed. Disregarding their voice or dominating the conversation with our monologues and rapid-fire speeches hinders communication; it doesn't encourage it.

Also, the mid-teen years are an especially important time to make your children feel they have a say in their lives. One way to accomplish this is by allowing them to have some ownership, with accountability, over less-weighty areas. Although we will continue to make the major decisions for them, there may be times when you can safely go along with a choice of theirs that you usually wouldn't, giving them a measured sense of autonomy. There may even be times you allow a decision that has the potential to produce unfavorable, but never harmful, results, in order to teach them the power and consequences of their choices. The upside is that this will all take place while they are still under your watchful eye, guiding them the entire time.

Allowing your children to express their voices doesn't diminish yours. As a matter of fact, demonstrating that you value them in this way can cause your voice to appreciate in value and improve your relationship with your children. While you're still mom, you also become a trusted guide or, dare I say, friend.

~

This brings us to a hot topic. There are differing views on whether or not a parent should also be their child's friend. I used to be of the belief that "never the twain shall meet," until one day it dawned on me: who do my girls confide in most? Their friends! And what do friends do? They relate, share interests, take the time to listen, understand without judgment, accept you for who you are, and tell you the truth – to name a few. Since I was already doing the majority of these – with the exception of needing to brush up on the latest teen happenings and jargon – I was game. And so, I purposely set out to join my girls' friend ranks.

The friendship I established with my girls wasn't one where I sought the status of a peer or their bestie – that was never my intention. I aimed to be more of an advisor-type friend, creating a space where they felt comfortable sharing with me what they typically wouldn't share with "mom." I developed this aspect of our relationship after establishing boundaries, making sure not to lose sight of my responsibilities as their parent first. And, while undoubtedly not privy to all of their secrets, being a friend to my girls made way for free-flowing communication, enabling them to see me as someone other than old-school, unrelatable mom who just doesn't understand.

~

If we are to influence our children, we must first relate to them. By taking the time to listen and respect them, we reciprocate respect. You'll see that taking the time to hear them out and consider their point of view will prove satisfactory to your teen. Because mostly, that's all they really want.

Preparing to Take Flight

Giving our children space to flourish and watching them come into their own is gratifying, especially when we have intentionally taken the time to foster that growth.

~

This reminds me of a time when Justyce and her friend decided to go riding on their motor scooters. Justyce had received her scooter a few years prior and was proficient at operating it, but Nia had just gotten hers a couple of days earlier and hadn't ridden it because, according to her, it wasn't working. As a result, Justyce decided to allow Nia to ride her scooter while she opted for her other manual one. Nia jumped on, excited to finally ride, turned the power lever, and nothing happened. She tried a few more times and still – nothing. I stood aside and observed as Justyce went over to determine what the problem was. She discovered that Nia wasn't operating the scooter properly.

Justyce explained that it was necessary to prime the scooter with a couple of manual pushes first before turning the power lever. This news made Nia's day causing her to run home to share her excitement with her mom and dad. Come to find out, her parents had planned to return her scooter to the store, concluding it was a lemon, not realizing that she was operating it incorrectly.

~

I later saw both Justyce and Nia outside, happily riding their motorized scooters up and down the street. To top it off, Nia wore a pink cape that flowed in the wind behind her. I noticed the confidence in their demeanors as they glided up and down the street. Seeing them brought a smile to my face.

I imagine that had I asked them how they felt that day, they probably would have said something like, "We're flying high!" Not only because Nia was finally able to ride her scooter, but more so because *they* were allowed to discover the solution, which made their experience all the more rewarding. Isn't that the cry of every child's heart – the freedom to let them do it on their own?

5

On Being Selfish (AKA Caring for Yourself)

Parenting is often considered a selfless job, where routinely putting our children and their interests first is lauded, while doing otherwise is deemed selfish. We've been made to believe that the more sacrificial our actions are toward our children, the better moms we are. It is this very belief that has hijacked the lives of so many of us.

While there will be plenty of times when you'll forgo personal gratification for the sake of benefiting your children, the downside of making this an indiscriminate habit is that you begin to disregard yourself while catering to their every whim.

Identity Theft –
Losing Ourselves in Them

Theft is an unfortunate yet daily reality we face in our world. Every object we own and deem even somewhat valuable has an alarm or lock affixed to it. Protective measures are taken to ensure our homes, cars, laptops, cell phones, and even our bikes are securely kept.

With all of this effort given to the safeguarding of our material goods from those with sticky fingers, we practically hand over one of our most valuable possessions to our children without a fight. What is it that I'm referring to, you ask? Our identity. Being a mom is many splendid things; one thing it isn't intended to be an abandonment of who we are as women.

Misplaced identity – becoming so immersed in our role as moms that we lose sight of who we are – is something that often takes place when adding "mom" to our title.

~

It occurs slowly, even undetectably at times, and then one day you look in the mirror and hardly recognize the reflection staring back at you. You've become lost amid bottles, diapers, schoolwork, kiddie shows, and activities, otherwise known as your child's world. The thing is, there are no alarms to alert you of this invasion.

As with any significant life change, having children requires adjustments, and a natural shifting of focus onto your child is sure to occur. This new focus can become so consuming that some moms forget to return their attention to themselves. It can get to the point where even the slightest thought of doing anything for or by yourself can conjure up guilty feelings of unfaithfulness to the call of motherhood. Unless recognized and nipped in the bud, this unexpected takeover can continue for years.

~

Why do so many moms become so engrossed in their children that they lose themselves? One reason is whatever you regularly pour your energy into without taking time to replenish can, gradually, cause your light to fade. In other words, you become lost in what has your attention. This same principle also applies to those who lose themselves in other types of relationships or even occupations.

We can get so caught up in making sure that our children have everything they need and are on track to reach their optimum potential that we overlook the fact that we have an optimum level of potential to attain as well. The privilege of being a mom doesn't negate other purposes that are equally a part of our calling and worthy of our attention. To leave them unfulfilled is to leave a piece of ourselves unrealized.

~

"Mom" is a title that you will always bear. But, be that as it may, your identity didn't begin and doesn't end there. Being a mom is only one facet of who you are – not the whole. Yes, with children comes responsibility, which I'm not suggesting you neglect. What I am proposing, however, is that you become equally careful not to neglect yourself in the process.

As difficult as it might be, admitting that you're deserving of the same level of attention that you give to your child is no crime. Doing so, however, will require times when you'll have to appear "selfish." This selfishness has nothing to do with being self-centered and everything to do with caring for yourself. It's regularly stepping back from the busyness of life to check in on yourself and feed your soul – however that might look for you, be it vacationing solo, taking a bike ride, journaling, curling up with a book, or doing absolutely nothing.

By recognizing the importance of making yourself a priority and taking the time to invest in yourself, the guilt you feel for doing so will loosen.

Understanding Your Enemy

Defeating mommy guilt requires an understanding of its modus operandi – the way it operates. Most of us can spot the overt guilt trips that are instigated by others a mile away, allowing ourselves time to brace and respond accordingly. The guilt trips that we're more susceptible to, however, aren't those straightforward ones. Instead, they're the ones that seemingly creep up out of the blue.

Like most bullies, mommy guilt knows its prey. As such, it zeros in on your vulnerabilities, often using areas where you lack confidence or self-knowledge to its advantage. By causing you to believe the false yet convincing allegations it fires off in your direction, it pulls you in hook, line, and sinker. These accusations don't usually come dressed as an obvious enemy, however – that would make them too easy to spot. Instead, they originate within your own heart, revealing an accuser more insidious than the one you're aware of. An accuser you don't expect: you.

We want to silence these false claims and reject the criticizing thoughts that surface in their wake. In this instance, however, the fabulist and its silencer are one and the same – you! That's right, dual roles. So, how can this be done? First off, you cannot refute a lie without knowing the truth. Therefore, defense against the accusations calls for firm knowledge of the one being accused – again, you. Once you're able to overcome and silence the attacks that originate within your own heart, conquering the ones from outside sources will be a piece of cake.

Getting to Know . . . You

It's said that knowledge is power. If that's true then two simple words that advise us to "know thyself" have the potential to change the way we combat the guilt that plagues us in the area of parenting.

Knowledge is information that's conveyed from one person to another, either through structured discussions, informal conversations, books, or other interactions. While these are all valid, attaining knowledge about yourself goes beyond these mediums. Although other people can provide clues, the actual work of achieving self-knowledge is a solo mission. And this is how it must be. Otherwise, allowing another to define you robs you of the confidence and personal power this knowledge yields.

~

It's common when asked to share something about ourselves to respond with the usual bullet points – name, where we live, occupation, and the like. And that's fine. We all start there. Plus, we wouldn't divulge intimate details to just anyone. But we short-change ourselves when we fail to dig deeper. The reality is, in our busy world, "get to know myself" isn't a top-ten item on many to-do lists. One reason being, most people are convinced they already have full knowledge of themselves, or at least know enough that there's no need for further inquiry. After all, you're you, so surely you know you, right? This isn't always the case. Being familiar with and genuinely knowing oneself are two different things. Unfortunately, many settle for the former and end up being a familiar stranger to themselves.

Getting to know someone or something doesn't happen by chance. To "know" is intimate. It's intentional. It requires effort. It's spending private, personal time with someone or something to increase knowledge. It's a willingness to uncover the good, the bad, and the ugly to reveal the true. The process of obtaining self-knowledge is no different. It isn't automatic; neither is it a once-and-done type thing where you do a bit of exploration, attain all there is to know about yourself, and then you're home free. No. We, like our children, are ever-changing, making this continual unfolding a recurring gift.

~

This brings us to the question: how well do you know yourself? I mean, *truly* know yourself. Where do you even begin such an inexhaustible search? A good starting point is to ask yourself direct questions geared toward gathering information about yourself. These questions will not only help you get to know yourself better, but they will cause you to recognize thought patterns that influence your behaviors, helping you to also understand the why behind the what – why you do what you do. Questions like:

- What do I like and dislike, and why?
- What do I believe or doubt, and why?
- Are my beliefs purely mine or merely passed down from others?
- What causes my mannerisms to change around certain people?
- What stirs my emotions – negatively or positively?
- What motivates my actions in certain situations?
- What brings me joy or makes me feel alive?
- What are my strengths and weaknesses?
- Do I put myself in positions to excel in my strengths and not to be overcome by my weaknesses?

- Why does this person (whoever "this" happens to be) annoy me?
- Why does being asked these types of questions irritate me?
- Why am I concerned about what other people think about me?

Use this limited list of basic questions to get started while continuing to add more probing ones that are specific to you. This exploration will help you go beyond the surface as you seek to uncover more of who you are.

~

Another approach is one I previously mentioned: check in with your senses. By paying attention to the different sensations your body experiences, you become familiar with your body's language. For example, what message is your gut communicating when you feel uneasy around certain people? What does the excitement you feel when in certain surroundings mean? These signals are sometimes dismissed as meaningless, when it's a higher part of our self communicating with and assisting us. While some individuals have developed this ability more than others, we are all capable of experiencing it in a way that becomes a real source of insight.

Giving heed to these areas – while also paying attention to what catches your glance, what excites you, the music that speaks to you, movies that inspire you, books that move you, as well as those things that repel or agitate you – prepares space where you can cultivate self-knowledge.

~

Many benefits make this quest of self-discovery more than worth your while. For one, you're sure to discover admirable attributes that you weren't aware of before. This knowledge will bring new understanding, appreciation, and self-love, ending the need to compare yourself to others. Plus, it will help you to unapologetically set boundaries that aid in maintaining your peace of mind. Additionally, the connectedness to oneself that this pursuit necessitates safeguards from becoming swept up in the identity-snatching whirlwind of parenting.

Along with the gains, you're bound to come face to face with some not-so-pleasant details that would be much easier to turn a blind eye to than sort through. This is an unavoidable part of the process and, to a great degree, is what you've signed up for, so don't let it throw you for a loop. Any unwanted conduct you desire to change must be revealed before it can be addressed. Some of these behaviors can be so ingrained that your awareness of them can often elude you.

Knowing how difficult confronting my shortcomings would be, I committed to practicing self-accountability: calling out my unacceptable behavior just as I would anyone else I cared about and loved. I love myself enough to be honest, even when it hurts. I became a diligent observer of my thoughts, actions, speech, attitudes, inner dialog, etc., always keeping a close friend or two with clearer filters in the wings to highlight blind spots I was oblivious to or to chime in when I was too emotionally connected to be objective. Progress came with much patience. By discontinuing patterns that fed unwanted behaviors, those habits were eventually starved out.

The question is, can you be honest with yourself without using what you learn against yourself? You know how we do: discover an area in our character or personality that we don't like and then commence to rail against ourselves. But this isn't about disliking what you find; it's about accepting what is and working through it. Also, being honest about and addressing what you learn about yourself isn't the same as being critical. We often conflate the two. However, criticism often takes the form of harsh, judgmental opinions offered without solutions, whereas honesty requires courage and kindness: courage to take ownership of your findings and kindness to be gentle with yourself as you do your work.

Self-knowledge equips you with the accurate information needed to counter the lies that attack from within and those that others aim your way. It strips the accuser of its power and places it back into the hands of its rightful owner – you! Thus, the advantage that self-knowledge provides is freedom from self-defeating thoughts, from the limiting opinions others have of you and that you have of yourself, and from negative behaviors you've believed to be true expressions of who you are.

~

Becoming free of mommy guilt also requires accepting yourself. We live in a time when dissatisfaction with oneself is widespread. Instead of investing in and learning to love the skin we're in, some individuals elect to take the path of least resistance by adapting their conduct or outer image to what public opinion or their tribe has deemed acceptable. Living falsely in this way fuels the frustration, confusion, and guilt many moms experience.

Self-acceptance is embracing the person you currently are as you continue to work towards becoming who you were created to be. Some of us may find it hard to believe that we can fully accept and even love ourselves before attaining the sought-after best version of ourselves that we're pursuing. Just as we love and accept our children as they grow, flaws and all, with the understanding that they're a work in progress, we are to do the same for ourselves. It isn't necessary for fruit to be visible on the tree for the tree to be enjoyed.

~

The point of this "cleaning house" isn't to spend your time sitting around navel-gazing. It's an invitation to rid yourself of thoughts, beliefs, and behaviors that contribute to the internal clutter of guilt and other patterns that don't benefit you. The ability to own up to your imperfections will provide an additional bonus: a humbling effect that makes you gentle not only with yourself but with other moms as well. When you realize we're all on the same journey, you'll begin to see them through a more compassionate and less judgmental lens.

~

The responsibility we have to know ourselves is a sacred calling. Failure to know is irreverent. By neglecting to explore yourself beyond the surface, you miss out on genuinely discovering and appreciating all that makes you, you. But you're not the only one robbed; you also deprive others of the opportunity to experience your truest expression. The metamorphosis that a butterfly undergoes is similar to the type of transformation that can potentially take place in our lives – if we embrace the process, that is.

Should I Stay or Should I Go – The Great Debate

There has been a long-standing debate between moms over whether being a stay-at-home mom or a mom who works outside of the home is most beneficial. Media outlets often find enjoyment in pitting these two groups against one another, chiming in with hollow discussions that are ineffective at best and troublesome at worst. Not to mention the depreciation our culture has for moms who stay home and the shame it heaps on moms who work. We're damned if we do, and damned if we don't.

Acknowledging what we already know to be true – that different families have different needs, thus necessitating different modes of operating – can put an end to these disputes. We're on the same team, only playing different positions.

The mom who elects to stay home most often does so because she believes she's the best candidate to look after and raise her children. And it's true: no one will nurture your child quite the way you do. Additionally, either she's financially able to do so, or she's made lifestyle adjustments to make it work.

Reasons abound as to why the mom who chooses to work outside of the home does so. She may be the sole provider for her family, thus having no other option. Or she's in a dual-income household where her pay is needed to make ends meet. Another mom might be more career-focused and simply enjoy what she does, while still another feels she doesn't possess the disposition, patience, or desire to stay home with her children all day.

Having occupied both positions, I can attest to the benefits and obstacles of both. I was unpleasantly surprised to learn, however, that the guilt was just as consuming whether I was home or working. As a stay-at-home mom, it was self-projected, whereas it was prompted by outside circumstances when I worked.

~

Staying home allowed me to participate in my girls' lives in an unrestricted way. Actively attending to the daily happenings of our household prevented situations that could have otherwise gone unnoticed from slipping through the cracks. Surprisingly, my family wasn't the only beneficiaries; staying home also had an unexpected effect on me. Freeing my mind from the demands of my job created space for unrealized talents, abilities, and even desires to surface. I'm convinced, had I not heeded the guidance to leave my job, you wouldn't be reading this book today. This isn't to say that everyone must quit their job to realize these things; that's just how it happened for me.

The guilt I experienced while staying home showed up mainly in the area of finances. Having always been independent and accustomed to having an income to contribute to our family, giving that up (albeit temporarily) was a huge hurdle I had to clear. I initially felt guilty about my inability to provide financially to our household, especially when money was tight. This eventually trickled over into feeling guilty for not being able to splurge from time to time on some of my girls' desires. Then came the guilt for feeling I had "wasted" my college degree; mainly when the work I performed at home was viewed as less than a real job, or when I felt less than appreciated.

On the other hand, working boosted my morale, served as an outlet for service to others and sociability for myself, and was, of course, a means to contribute financially to my family.

Yet, working occupied the most and best hours of my day to such a degree that I often battled with slight feelings of neglecting my girls. That, plus the mental exhaustion I experienced from working interfered, at times, with the quality of attention I was able to give them. This caused me to experience guilt in the areas of time and attention. There were even moments when I contemplated withholding needed discipline from them when feelings of guilt about the amount of time (physically and mentally) that I spent away from them crept up. Although I earned a good salary, I concluded it wasn't worth the exchange for the version of myself I brought home to my family each night neither was it fair to them.

In a nutshell – as a stay-at-home mom, I felt guilty about not working, and as a working mom, I felt guilty about working.

~

Deciding to stay home with my children or work outside of the home turned out to be a trade-off of sorts: either trading dollars for time or trading time for dollars. In both instances, I weighed my options, made clear my intent, and moved forward. As a stay-at-home mom, if I could reconcile not being able, for a season, to contribute financially or treat my girls to a few wants with being available to pour into the lives of my girls in an intentional, unrestricted way – all while maintaining my identity – I succeeded. And if, as a working mom, I accepted that, while there would be times when my girls would be adversely affected by my time constraints, so long as I was able to successfully disconnect from my work to spend real quality time with them when it was called for, meant I'd have succeeded there as well. Also, nothing was etched in stone. I could revisit my decision at any time.

Coming to terms with this not only held guilt at bay but also allowed my experience as both a stay-at-home mom and a working mom to be more rewarding.

~

It goes without saying that both of these approaches are valid and each is beneficial in its own way; neither needs qualifying. They both require work, only different kinds. Both provide pay, only with different currencies. Both require intentionality seeing that if you're not careful, you can lose connection to yourself or your child in either one.

I'm convinced that if we had our way, we would love to have our cake and eat it too – choosing to be a full-time mom to our children while pursuing a career we love. This may be why the stay-at-home mom tries her hand at entrepreneurship – not only to earn an income but also to put her talents to use. It also explains why the working mom busts her butt to participate in as many of her children's events as possible so as to not leave the impression that she wasn't present.

~

I'll close this section with an account that underscores the pointlessness of this debate. A mom shared with me how she often felt looked down upon by the stay-at-home moms at her daughter's school because she worked a great deal. While attending a Girl Scouts event, one of those moms said to her, "You think we [stay-at-home moms] have our act together more than we do." That moment of honesty changed the working moms point of view, causing her to appreciate moms who were able to stay home. She realized that without those stay-at-home moms volunteering for many of the kids' activities that working moms couldn't possibly add to their schedules, her child and many other children would miss out on a number of valuable experiences.

In the final analysis, all moms want only the best for their children and are doing the best they can to provide such. Regardless of our current mom position, let us stop throwing jabs at each other and start rooting for one another, ending this futile debate. Imagine the powerful team we could forge if we were to put aside our "us versus them" mentality and join forces. Instead, becoming a part of the village we often hear is needed to raise children.

6

A Spiritual Take on Things

Many people consider parenting one of the most, if not *the* most, important role a person can assume. Taking on the endless task of guiding, navigating, and making decisions for someone else's life, especially the life of a child, is a tremendous responsibility. And yet, we aren't given a how-to tutorial on getting it right upon leaving the hospital. Instead, it's a skill that's learned as we go along.

Could the fact that this incredible assignment that doesn't come with instructions indicate there is no set right or wrong way to do it, generally speaking? That just as there are billions of people with a vast array of personalities and perspectives, there are also various methods of parenting that will produce responsible, productive, caring human beings?

Finding ourselves in a parental pickle can have us seeking advice from family, friends, and even strangers with hopes that parenting techniques they've found successful will prove useful for us as well. Sometimes those techniques work, other times not. Why the inconsistency? Simply because the children in question are all different, bringing about varying results.

As such, an individualized approach is needed when it comes to raising individuals. This is the part of parenting that required I tuned in to a Higher Source for direction concerning my children.

~

As I alluded to in the beginning, spirituality played a significant role in freeing me from mommy guilt, mainly by changing my perception of my girls. Although their physical makeup shouted that they were children, subject to my leadership who I was to protect, mold, and ensure their lives turn out correctly, I began to understand they were much more than that. They were as much spiritual in nature as they were human. Both of them were sent here with a specific, drafted blueprint, and understanding it only required that I sought counsel from the Architect who created the design. This was a realization I've had to remind myself of more than a few times along the way.

My children came through me but didn't belong to me. In other words, they weren't mine to do with as I pleased. They were entrusted to me (and Franklin) to guide in natural and spiritual matters until they developed the ability to tune into their internal guidance systems on their own. And, while I knew this conceptually, I often behaved otherwise.

This humbling insight not only shifted the way I viewed my girls, but also altered every aspect of how I interacted with them. I went from parenting from a place of ownership and fear to trusting the guidance of the Divine Source that abided within them and myself, which was more than able to guide us as we journeyed on this path of life together.

But let's back up a bit to where I was before gaining this understanding.

Parenting . . . A Spiritual Endeavour

Prior to becoming a mom, I thought I was a parenting expert. After watching many moms struggle to get their children to obey, behave, or simply have a decent relationship with them, I vowed that wouldn't be my story. With my experience in babysitting, working with children at schools, and leading a few youth groups under my belt, I was ready. I would run a tight ship and make clear what behavior would and wouldn't be accepted. They would listen, respect me, and that would be that. I mean, how hard could it be?

But, as I said, that was *before* I became a mom. My actual induction into Tribe Mommy would turn my world upside-down.

~

Having never carried a child of my own, I failed to understand the bond I would develop with each of my children in those nine months. It would be a connection that would significantly grow once I saw my girls face to face. How could these little six-pound babies command, even *demand*, so much without being able to verbalize a single word? Emotions that I'd never experienced arose and concerns I'd never entertained filled my thoughts.

Needless to say, all of my preconceived mommy notions were tossed out of the window as I quickly learned there was a marked difference between relating to my children and someone else's. I experienced first-hand the decision-making quandary moms faced on a daily basis. Choices that weren't always as clear-cut as I'd presumed. This realization brought newfound respect that led me to send a virtual apology to all the moms I had silently (and at times not so silently) and so amateurishly criticized in the past.

~

The relationships we have with our children are filled with highs and lows. These phases can produce just the right amount of pressure necessary for the maturity and evolution of both child and parent – if we allow them to. Going through these phases with my girls opened my eyes to just how much of a spiritual journey parenting is. Think about it. How could a relationship this intricate and responsibility of such magnitude be otherwise? I often faced challenges where the answers weren't Googleable. I needed help. I needed divine wisdom.

~

To view parenting as a divinely inspired appointment implies being specifically chosen and thus well suited for the task. It's an appointment that's intentional, purposeful, and, dare I say, maybe even prearranged. Understanding this spiritual dynamic of parenting has the potential to alleviate much of the conflict we encounter, especially as our children mature. This view might be a new concept for some individuals. But hang in there with me while I explain.

A Match Made in Heaven

I've often heard it said that "you can't choose your parents," which, for the longest time, led me to believe that the pairing of parents and children was a decision that we're completely removed from. Instead, I thought, it was solely determined by God or, at least, by the sperm that reached the egg first. I also believed that circumstances such as being born to affluent parents or your child being a wunderkind were as much the luck of the draw, so to speak, as being born to needy parents or finding that your child has learning challenges. This was the case until a friend of mine shared something that her three-year-old said that caused me to reconsider my belief.

~

My friend mentioned how she'd expressed to her young daughter how happy she was to be her mom, to which her daughter matter-of-factly replied, "I know, that's why we picked each other." My friend, a bit baffled, continued by inquiring as to what she meant. Her daughter went on to say, "Remember? We picked each other before we got here. I told you I wanted you to be my mom, and you told me you wanted me to be your little girl. We picked each other."

Well, of course, my friend didn't have any recollection of this conversation, but her daughter was certain it took place. My friend shared that, once she recovered from astonishment, she committed that exchange with her daughter to memory, which is exactly what I did.

~

Some doubting Thomasinas might chalk this up to pure childhood fantasy. Possibly. I'd read stories told by other young children who recalled similar occurrences. But this was different; it was coming from someone I knew, someone who wasn't known for this type of otherworldly talk, so it arrested my attention. That and I tend to listen to the farfetched stories children tell. Maybe it's because, as a child, I, too was a teller of similar narratives that actually took place but were dismissed after being attributed to my overactive imagination.

Naturally, my curious mind began racing. What if this was true, and we did have a say in the details of our life before arriving here? And, like everything else in our sagacious universe, the children you have weren't arbitrary. But the circumstances that made it possible for any of us to be here were meticulously planned, leaving "chance" or "accidents" out of the equation. That would be a game-changer.

An arrangement of such intentionality would imply that the lessons our children come to teach us are as vital in helping us to develop as the ones we teach them. It would also call for a higher level of accountability. Not only are they accountable to us, but we are equally accountable to them. We thereby expand the scope of our relationship with our children into a partnership as we jointly work to fulfill our individual and collective purposes.

~

Our Divine Source doesn't bring us here and give us life to then leave us to our own devices. But, just as the plans for our entry were orchestrated, so are our subsequent life plans. The choice is ours as to whether we'll connect to that Higher Wisdom and discover those plans or take a different path.

While this doesn't permit us to throw caution to the wind, citing, "what will be will be," it does free us from carrying the burdensome belief that the destiny and fate of our children rest completely in our laps. It also assures us that, as we consciously go through our days connecting to and acknowledging our Divine Source while making mindful decisions for our children, and ourselves, our lives unfold as they should.

Approaching parenting from the understanding that I had a Helper assisting me every step of the way removed much of the pressure, fear, and guilt of mothering mistakes and freed me to relish in the journey.

Some moms might feel ill-equipped to lead their children in this way. The truth is you're already doing it to some degree. How, you ask? Purely by being their parent. Allow me to elaborate.

Their Eyes Are Watching

Certain events of my youth are etched in my memory. One such incident took place, once again, at church. But before I get into that, a little history. As a child, the adoration and love I held for my mother were abundant (and still are). From my perspective, she was perfect, second to none, could do no wrong – you catch my drift.

One particular Sunday, the pastor shared how God requires us to love Him more than any other person or thing, which, to me, translated to my mom. I'm sure there was more to the message; however, he lost my attention after that statement. As you can imagine, hearing this sent me into a tizzy – what had been said seemed utterly irrational to my then eight-year-old comprehension. While I understood the concept of God, the relationship I had with my mom was tangible and far exceeded any connection I had established with God.

I remember my mind flooding with a series of questions: *Is he serious? How can I love God more than my mom? Does God really expect this from me? That's crazy! I can't even see God; He doesn't even talk to me, so how does He expect me to love Him the most?! I want to get into Heaven, but will I be able to if I don't love God the most? Hell is hot! Ugh!* *Frown*

~

My understanding of this matter has since matured, but here's my point; before your child attends any religious service or acquires any real grasp of who or what God is, you are the closest thing to God they know. Meaning, you're the first one they come to love completely, trust wholly, depend on fully, and admire utterly. That, plus you are the first person who displays godlike qualities to them by unconditionally loving, nurturing, and protecting them. This natural bond can inadvertently cause them to esteem you as godlike. But no need to worry – this estimation will correct itself in due time.

Additionally, you're the one your children instinctively take their cues from, making you their first teacher in both natural and spiritual matters. Thus, how you live your life becomes a constant illustration of the principles you adhere to. But unlike the lessons you purposely set out to teach them, these are more observational – e.g., the way you interact with others, your tone of voice when responding or reacting, your integrity behind closed doors, your character when under pressure. And as much as we'd like for our words to have the final say, the truth is it's our actions that carry the most influential weight. As such, your children are more inclined to imitate what you do than to merely follow what you say, proving actions really do speak louder than words, especially if the two are incongruent.

Parenting with a spiritual perspective helps us to see our children and our responsibility as moms through a broader lens. Viewing parenting this way came about as I sought ways to raise my girls with the love, support, and boundaries they needed, minus the many guilts and fears I often found myself entangled in. My search ended when it dawned on me to look to the One whose "parenting" record has been impeccable in my life – my Maker.

Which Way is Up?

As you can probably gather, I've spent my share of days attending church services. Of the many teachings, sermons, and stories I've heard over the years, there has always been one common thread woven throughout – God is love, and God's love toward us is unconditional, unceasing, and fervent. And while there were numerous occasions when God's children were rescued from dangers, there were other times when the divine hand of protection was slightly lifted, allowing God's children to taste the bitterness of hardship. These occasions included situations that we would expect any good parent to prevent. From this, I began to understand that God's way of doing things was the opposite of ours. God's right-side-up is often what we would consider upside-down.

I wasn't familiar with this expression of love. While it was a love that shielded, protected, and was abundantly generous, it was also a love displayed by one who didn't always avert challenges by stepping in to save the day but at times, granted them entrance, knowing they build character. A love demonstrated by one who understood that pressures of life are needed to extract the diamond within, thus gave consent to the heat. It's a love shown by one who allows wisdom to rule in decision-making, which, at times, requires a tempering of emotions and the inner strength to do all of this confidently and without feeling guilty about it.

This understanding led me to think: if God, our Divine Source, being all-wise, wholly good, and the epitome of love finds it necessary to allow difficulties in our lives, those difficulties must somehow be beneficial to our overall development.

Many of us equate love mostly with rescuing, protecting, and guarding our children against failure and discomfort, while at the same time indulging upon them their heart's desire. However, could allowing inconveniences and disappointments to play out be just as much an expression of love as our attempt to forbid the same? Now, I'm not suggesting we throw our children into a lion's den or toss them out to sea to be swallowed by a whale, but rather to consider the role that difficult times play in helping them build stamina and reach their maximum potential.

~

But that's God's way of doing things, and I'm not God. So, my question was, how would this look in my everyday life? The answer first shocked, then scared, but in the end liberated me.

Strong Love

When I was in my twenties, I often found myself torn between telling friends the truth about certain issues or withholding it so as not to hurt their feelings. Although they claimed to want the truth, I knew certain friends couldn't stomach it and that speaking honestly would have put a wedge between us. The majority of the time, I sided with preserving their feelings and our friendship. This produced a cycle of me holding my tongue, my friend continuing the behavior, and repeated aggravation that eventually strained the friendship. In the end, my attempt at keeping the peace did anything but.

It was around this same time that someone told me, "Dayna, you've got to learn how *not* to care, in order *to* (truly) care. Although I understood what this meant, having never practiced it, that understanding was only surface level. Years later, this piece of advice took on a deeper meaning, especially when it came to overcoming mommy guilt.

~

There's a fine line between caring about and loving someone or something, so fine that their meanings are often substituted. You can care without loving, but you can't love without also caring.

To care is to have an interest in the wellbeing of someone or the outcome of something. We care about many things; ourselves, our families, and our friends, as well as responsibilities such as work, our neighborhoods, the organizations we belong to, etc. But there's another side to caring, one that can tailspin into worry. This is where our minds crowd with anxious thoughts and cause us to become unsettled. This type of caring is often rooted in concern over situations that are out of our control.

Love, on the other hand, being the most powerful force in our universe, is confident, firm, and sure. Not the diluted, self-serving, sugary love we often see portrayed, but love in its fullest and purest sense – God's love.

Love is often thought of as deep feelings or affection, and it does include those things. But it's more than intense emotions. There is a side to love that's requiring. It's exhibiting patience, kindness, and understanding to others as well as to yourself. It's the ability to see yourself in others and, as such, to practice the golden rule of treating them as you would like to be treated.

~

It's said that God's love is most reflected in the love a mother has for her children. In a lot of ways, this is true in that it's unconditional, steadfast, undying, and fiery. There are few things a mother wouldn't do for her children. God's love, however, has levels and depths that greatly exceed ours as moms. It operates out of vast wisdom, omniscient knowledge, and a determined commitment to seeing us maximize our full potential.

While I won't pretend to comprehend the expansive scope of God's love fully, there is one word I like to use when describing it. That word is "strong." The image of a muscle-bound individual might have popped into your mind. However, the strength I'm referring to has nothing to do with being physically robust.

What exactly, then, is "strong love?" It's a mature love that cares intensely, yet, being anchored in reality and truth, isn't easily moved or disturbed by sentimentality. It's emotionally disciplined, meaning it makes space for the rise and expression of emotions without allowing them to take over. It's a love that's devoted and loyal, always doing what's best for the one it's extended toward. It's fearless. Being confident in the divine deposits made in each of us allows God to love us enough to set us free, while, at the same time, never completely letting us go.

Strong love operates from a higher vantage point. Decisions made from that altitude can, at times, appear irrational. The amount of pushback you're likely to encounter as a result of your child's inability to understand your rationale can make the execution of those decisions difficult. It's a love, however, that's willing to risk being misunderstood in the short-term to reap the long-term benefits of a child who matures responsibly.

To be effective, strong love must come from a soft heart that desires what's best for your children in every situation. When initially and correctly executed, you can be sure that guilt will be lurking nearby, ready to pounce. However, having total confidence and remaining secure in the decisions you make for your children can halt guilt in its tracks.

~

This expression of love differed from what I displayed, yet I knew it best modeled how I should lead my girls as they matured. But did I have what it took to carry it out? As I grappled with this, I became aware of another noteworthy characteristic of God's love – its deeply intimate yet paradoxically impersonal nature.

Impersonal Parenting

Of the many areas that moms listed as guilt triggers, the second most common cause of mommy guilt, after lack of time, was guilt that arises during times of conflict and discipline. You know, those times when you and your children don't quite see eye-to-eye.

As moms, nothing brings us joy quite like seeing our children happy. Watching their faces light up with delight is a high like no other. By the same token, nothing dampens our mood the way seeing them sad does. Ironically, there are times when we're the producer of those unhappy faces, also making us the recipient of their poked lips and sour moods. For some moms, the thought of encountering such reactions from their children is enough to deter them from confronting difficult issues as their way of attempting to maintain peace. True peace isn't gained or sustained by the absence of conflict, but by addressing the very issue that threatens to disturb it.

Knowing that disappointing my children would be impossible to avoid, I surmised there were many pouts, snarls, and tears in our future through which I would have to endure. Doing this successfully would require becoming immune to the reactions some of my choices were sure to ignite in them. It also called for controlling my emotions in a way that allowed me to address the situations clearheaded.

This is where that bit of advice I received years earlier paid off. By caring less – about their disagreeing outbursts over decisions I made for them or about whether they'll still love me after making said decisions – I was able to continue with decisions that were difficult to implement, yet what I knew was right. This was the answer to helping me weather their fits and frets – minus the guilt.

Impersonal parenting is the ability to temporarily detach your emotions from difficult parenting situations that create feelings of mommy guilt. By learning not to take those situations personally, you're able to approach them as objectively as possible - free from the sway of your child's opposition. Success at this requires the pre-work of emotional discipline, which we'll discuss shortly.

~

Although some people believe that any expression of emotion is a sign of weakness, it isn't. To connect with our feelings is to be in touch with our humanity. Emotions are purposeful, needed, and aren't, in and of themselves, the issue. The problem occurs when we fail to discipline our emotions. If we were to recall some of our biggest regrets, we'd probably find they occurred when our raw emotions were in control. Allowing our undisciplined emotions to drive our decisions, especially in stirring situations, has a way of fogging our perception, resulting in us misclassifying our actions, or lack thereof, as love.

We're clearest in our thinking, surer in our actions, and most honest in our advice when not being led by our undisciplined emotions. Think about times you've given sound advice to a friend. Chances are, you were able to do so because you weren't directly affected by the situation. Simply put, your emotions were detached or at least less involved than the individual in the thick of it. In like manner, when faced with a situation where guilt looms and the ability to gain proper perspective eludes you, ask yourself, "How would I advise a friend in this same predicament?" In other words, pretend you're the one giving the advice instead of the one receiving it. Help offered from that frame of mind is usually the most honest. If the advice you would offer a friend is acceptable for them to follow, it should be adequate for you to heed as well. This little role-play has saved me from many brushes with mommy guilt.

Another creative mental exercise to try when feelings of guilt and emotional proximity makes it difficult to follow-through with disciplining your child is to imagine the person before you as someone other than your child. This should be someone you're not as emotionally attached to, yet someone you want the best for, such as another family member or the child of a close friend. What would you tell her or him? This can sometimes make proceeding with your decision a bit easier.

Isn't it interesting how we always know just what someone else's child needs?

A sports commentator provided an excellent example of this very concept. In 2015, Venus and Serena Williams went head to head during the US Open quarterfinals match. With the two of them having such a close relationship, people questioned whether they would be able to play to the best of their abilities without one feeling guilty about defeating the other. The commentator stated it would be vital for them not to view one another as sisters so as to keep the result they were attempting to achieve at the forefront of their minds. As I watched, I observed how the sisters disengaged themselves from their usual close, jovial relationship, instead taking on the roles of mere opponents, keeping their individual goals in view. I particularly noticed how Serena went a step further and purposely avoided making eye contact with Venus throughout the entire match. And she pulled out the victory in the end!

Granted, walking this out with a sibling on a world stage with thousands of screaming fans is a bit different than it would be in your living room with your screaming, angry child, but the execution is the same.

~

Practicing healthy detachment during times of conflict, particularly during times of discipline, has nothing to do with disconnecting from your children or withholding love, compassion, or attention from them. Instead, it honors your children and your commitment to helping them reach their full potential by following through with what you know will be most beneficial for them in the long run. Although possibly gut-wrenching in the moment, this type of detachment places the relationship we have with them in proper perspective by allowing us to see the bigger picture.

Something else it does is put the emotional bond we have with our children in its rightful place. It reminds us to hold them close but with relaxed fingers, because they, like us, have an individual path to traverse – a journey where we're their guide for only a short time. As such, we're here to teach them and, little by little, release them onto that path; or as I once heard it put, "guide and step aside." This, in turn, releases us from the exhausting task of trying to control every aspect of their lives and relieves them from the pressure of fulfilling our innumerable expectations – making room for fuller enjoyment in the relationship. But rather than gradually loosening our grip, it often tends to become more fastened (or attached) over time, resulting instead in us needing to have our fingers pried from our children's lives.

Implementing strong love and operating from a place of healthy emotional detachment isn't for the faint of heart. Incorporating those two elements, along with an understanding of the spiritual nature of my relationship with my girls, set me on the path of eradicating mommy guilt from my life. For me, getting to this place was far from an overnight success. Like any worthwhile change, it required work. And the will to attain and maintain my freedom began with and continues to depend on me.

~

Our journey to becoming free from mommy guilt has taken us down many avenues, all of which are more than capable of dousing guilt's fire. I must say, however, that overcoming mommy guilt in one phase of motherhood doesn't automatically mean you'll avoid it in other phases. If you're not careful, the ground you've gained can be lost. To ensure that not one ember remains hot enough to rekindle, I've saved the most important tools for last. Once harnessed, these are sure to dismantle mommy guilt of its power once and for all.

Soul Strength

Living in a way that focuses mainly on ensuring all of our external I's are dotted and T's crossed encourages the perpetuation of mommy guilt. This often results in us leaving the most crucial part of ourselves that's hidden from the naked eye undeveloped and vulnerable; our soul.

Not to be confused with your spirit, which is the infinite part of your makeup that's connected to God and makes connecting with God possible, your soul is your immaterial essence that consists of your mind, emotions, and will. It's a mixture of positive and negative tendencies, along with mental and behavioral patterns and experiences you acquire throughout life. It's also from where your personality and ego stems and what differentiates you from every other human being. Simply put, it's what makes you, you. The condition of your soul contributes greatly to the overall quality of your life.

~

Mommy guilt is a feeling: an emotion. Like all emotions, it initiates in the soul then rises to the conscious level, eventually showing up in our behaviors. In other words, it operates from the inside out. Just as I found it interesting that moms are the most inclined to this type of parental guilt, I also wondered why mommy guilt has such a high success rate at tormenting so many of us. We experience a multitude of feelings and emotions daily, so what is it about this particular emotion that plagues us the way that it does?

Then it hit me: the heart of a mother is to nurture and protect. We want our children to lead fulfilled lives, which is why we spend countless hours equipping, instructing, and instilling in them valuable lessons. As such, we naturally assume a greater sense of responsibility for their development and often take the outcomes of their lives more personally. To the same degree that we pat ourselves on the back for their successes and bask in the accolades we receive in regards to parenting them, we guilt ourselves for their letdowns and our parenting mishaps.

This hurricane of activity takes place in our minds (thoughts), affects our emotions (feelings), and influence our will (decisions), making clear the reason why mommy guilt thrives. We've failed to establish defenses where it originates: internally. More specifically, we've neglected to strengthen our soul.

~

The soul is innately strong, meaning it has what's needed to overcome adversities and setbacks. However, the social conditioning, criticisms, offenses, abuses, doubts, fears, etc. that we experience in life, as well as the emotional reactions those experiences trigger, can weaken its strength over time, resulting in the formation of a bruised ego.

Just as we strengthen our physical bodies with proper nutrition, exercise, and adequate rest, our souls are a part of our spiritual makeup that requires appropriate nurture and care as well. It just so happens that your bruised ego plays an essential role in strengthening your soul. Identifying what sets it off reveals the wounded areas of your soul that are in need of healing. By addressing those areas and giving them the necessary time and attention to heal, you progressively reclaim and strengthen that part of your soul, ultimately healing the bruised ego and silencing your inner mean girl. As such, strengthening the soul requires fortifying its various components – mind, emotions, and will.

Tough Mind

Mommy-guilty thoughts can turn habit-forming over time, becoming our automatic mental responses in guilt-inducing situations. As with any unwanted habit, these thought patterns die hard. There can even be times as you're making progress when you begin to feel guilty for *not* feeling guilty. Crazy! Conflicting feelings such as this is evidence that the bruised ego is healing yet still trying to hold on for dear life. You'll have the choice of either aligning with those thoughts and feelings when they surface or seeing them for the lies that they are. They will eventually lose their hold, but not without a fight.

Although other people can participate in infecting you with these mommy-guilty thoughts, your beef isn't mostly with them; neither does this conflict play out in the view of others. Instead, it takes place right between your ears: on the battlefield of your mind – and the battle real. Warring against yourself might seem counterintuitive and counterproductive; however, this battle isn't meant to destroy your mind but to toughen it, thereby cultivating mental stamina.

~

There's a proverb that advises to "be careful of what you think because your thoughts control your life," or, stated another way, "as you think, so are you." These two potent sayings give clues as to just how closely linked our life experiences are to our thoughts. This places the onus on us to pay attention to our thoughts. The flow of our life – how peaceful or chaotic it is – is a direct result of our dominant thoughts. It could even be said that the outward expression of someone's life is a manifestation of that individual's inner thoughts.

A tough mind has expanded beyond the confines of negative appraisals or the praise of flattery. And, having built up resistance by being independent of the opinions of other people, the tough-minded individual isn't easily unnerved or impressed by such assessments but is quick to reject these types of estimations. Such a mind doesn't appear out of thin air; it's deliberately sought, deliberately contended for.

~

How, exactly, do you toughen your mind? Allow me to share an example. When Jaicie was younger, I regularly styled her hair by parting it down the middle with a ponytail on each side. Over time, that part became fixed to the point that her hair began to naturally fall along that established parted line even when I didn't want it to. It took a while for me to retrain her hair to flow differently but, as I continued working on it, parting and styling it in new ways, her hair eventually adapted, and that middle part slowly faded. You establish a tough mind in the same manner – by retraining it to regularly and immediately interrupting the flow of negative, harassing, or unwanted thought patterns with healthy ones until a new "part" or way of thinking is formed in your mind.

Dwelling on any mommy guilt-inducing thought only strengthens the hold that thought has on you. Instead of rehearsing the allegation, realize who is speaking (bruised inner meanie) and interrupt her ramblings with the truth. Initially, you might feel crazy having this internal conversation, but after a while, she'll stop driving you crazy with her jibber-jabber.

Bolstering your mind with toughness is foundational for overcoming mommy guilt, but it's the first of a double-punch combination.

Emotional Discipline

Emotions – those beautiful yet messy, simple yet complex feelings that impact our mood, influence our behavior, and affect our health. These powerful sensations, that rise and fall in intensity, act as indicators of how we experience and interpret different events or situations that happen to or around us. How we respond to our emotions play a big part in the way we relate to them. And our response is entirely our choice. Just as it's essential to toughen our minds, it's important to discipline our emotions, or more accurately, our responses to emotional impulses, if we are to live free of mommy guilt.

Emotional discipline - adept at effectively managing our emotions - begins with recognizing what triggers mommy guilt within us. Understanding what's taking place when we're triggered helps us to better handle those occurrences. Disciplining our emotions also involves choosing to display emotions that are beneficial and refusing to regularly display those that aren't. I refer to these as higher and lower emotions. Their classification is indicative of their effects. Higher, more beneficial emotions are love, peace, joy, patience, gratitude, and compassion, and a few of the lower ones include shame, jealousy, blame, fear, envy, and worry.

While higher emotions are more productive, operating in them often requires focused intentionality. As such, displaying them doesn't always come easy. There will be times you won't necessarily *feel* like being patient or kind to others – you choose to do so despite how you feel. You'll find that the more you elect higher emotions, the more natural those responses will become. If operating in the higher emotions isn't your norm, time will be needed to change the lifelong behavioral patterns you've established. As such, don't give up if you aren't able to master it right out of the gate. It's a journey where change happens bit by bit.

~

The emotions most often felt by moms who struggle with mommy guilt fit into the lower emotions category. They include, of course, guilt (trips), doubt, regret, fear, judgment, and shame. Although these emotions result in unpleasant mental experiences, we shouldn't ignore them, beat ourselves up for feeling them, or deny what we feel. Instead, we should acknowledge them and allow the unpleasantness they generate to point out areas within us that need addressing.

Having a strategy for handling lower emotions when they appear can give us an advantage over them. Whether that strategy includes pausing to think before we respond, walking away to gather ourselves, or examining the situation to determine if the guilt we're experiencing is legitimate or illusory – a controlled response is always better than an impulsive reaction.

~

Whether you're aspiring to genuinely display higher emotions or wanting to eliminate lower ones, help from a Source higher than mere willpower is required. Accessing this divine assistance starts by humbling yourself and earnestly asking for it. Acknowledging your need, positions you to receive guidance and grace. Follow this up with adopting practices that align with your goal and eliminating contrary ones.

Your success at becoming and remaining free from mommy guilt depends on your ability to replace your established reactions with disciplined responses. When your tough mind teams up with your disciplined emotions to make willed decisions through the lens of strong, unconditional love, you have an equation for real confidence in parenting and in life.

Final Thoughts

You might be thinking, *All of this to become free from mommy guilt?* Yes! Mommy guilt is an assault on the worth, ability, confidence, contribution, and esteem of moms. Ceasing to view it as something that we must tolerate and beginning to see it for the antagonist it is changes our position from being its victim to being the victor over it.

Becoming a guilt-free mom requires letting go as well as embracing: letting go of your ideal mothering image and embracing who you indeed are as a mom; letting go of unrealistic expectations you hold your children to and embracing their actual capabilities. It's the process of changing internally so that your external experience as a mom changes for the better as well.

~

Everything we've discussed – confidence in parenting, refusing to compete and compare, disregarding the opinion of others, forgiving yourself for parenting mistakes, knowing yourself, etc. – are tools to assist you in overcoming mommy guilt. Still, claiming your freedom can only be fully realized by purposeful pursuit.

The good news is that you're not alone in your pursuance. We're all in this together. You have the wind of countless other moms at your back, including me, rooting for your freedom! More importantly, you have a Source within who provides strength far superior to anything anyone can give or that you can produce on your own. So, when you're at the point where you've done all you can, surrender to the One who knows all, understands all, and can bring resolution to it all.

Being a mom is a weighty responsibility for sure, but it can also be an amazing, lesson-filled adventure. Let's start to more fully embrace the latter by learning from our children in the way they live life fully, in the moment, and guilt-free.

Yeah . . . let's do that.

 *Dayna*

Made in the USA
Coppell, TX
23 July 2020

31615468R00094